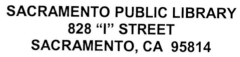

Guide to

Easy HOME
IMPROVEMENT

The

Guide to

Easy **HOME**
IMPROVEMENT

Paige Hemmis

A PLUME BOOK

PLUME
Published by the Penguin Group
Penguin Group (USA) Inc., 375 Hudson Street, New York, New York 10014,
U.S.A. • Penguin Group (Canada), 90 Eglinton Avenue East, Suite 700, Toronto,
Ontario, Canada M4P 2Y3 (a division of Pearson Penguin Canada Inc.) • Penguin
Books Ltd., 80 Strand, London WC2R 0RL, England • Penguin Ireland, 25 St.
Stephen's Green, Dublin 2, Ireland (a division of Penguin Books Ltd.) • Penguin
Group (Australia), 250 Camberwell Road, Camberwell, Victoria 3124, Australia (a
division of Pearson Australia Group Pty. Ltd.) • Penguin Books India Pvt. Ltd., 11
Community Centre, Panchsheel Park, New Delhi – 110 017, India • Penguin Books
(NZ), cnr Airborne and Rosedale Roads, Albany, Auckland 1310, New Zealand (a di-
vision of Pearson New Zealand Ltd.) • Penguin Books (South Africa) (Pty.) Ltd., 24
Sturdee Avenue, Rosebank, Johannesburg 2196, South Africa

Penguin Books Ltd., Registered Offices: 80 Strand, London WC2R 0RL, England

First published by Plume, a member of Penguin Group (USA) Inc.

First Printing, December 2006
10 9 8 7 6 5 4 3 2 1

LIBRARY OF CONGRESS CATALOGING-IN-PUBLICATION DATA

Hemmis, Paige.
    The tuff chix guide to easy home improvement / Paige Hemmis
        p.   cm.
    "A Plume Book."
    Includes index.
    ISBN 0-452-28761-8
1. Dwellings—Maintenance and repair—Amateurs' Manuals.   I. Title.

TH4817.3.H46 2006
643'.7—dc22

2006027186

Printed in the United States of America
Set in Fairfield Medium
Designed by Helene Berinsky

This book is dedicated to the true Tuff Chix in my life: my mom, Karel; my grandmother, Joyce "Dimmy"; and my stepmom, Joy. Without the support and guidance of these amazing women, who all shared their tools of life with me, I would not be the person (or the Tuff Chick) that I am today.

This book is also dedicated to the Tuff Chix of the future: Zoey, Harley, and Presley Novak, who have touched my heart and changed my life forever.

Acknowledgments

Writing this book has been a labor of love that *definitely* could not have been completed without the support, love, and friendship of my business partner and publicist, Angela Moore of Starfish PR. Any time of day or night, she is there for me, and she is more appreciated than words can describe. The same is true for my business partner, cousin, partner in crime, and true friend, Jaime Britz, who has been my soul mate and inspiration since the day she was born. I thank my brother and closest friend, Michael Huff, who continues to inspire me day after day with achieving so much at such a young age, and is there for me when I need advice, need a friend, or just need a hug. I thank my dad, Larry "Soapy Sales" Huff, for passing along his passion of hard work, his entrepreneurial spirit, and his love of fast cars. I thank my grandma, Joyce "Dimmy" Thomson, who has led this family with love, grace, and honor. I thank my stepmom, Joy Jamieson, for teaching me how to be a strong, independent woman, and to love unconditionally in conditional situations.

I thank my mom, Karel Huff, who is so much more than just a mom—for everything she taught me throughout the years, and for every sacrifice she made to give my brother and me a great life, and for everything she continues to do for me today. Mama . . . YOU ARE THE BEST!

There are so many people who helped me, not only with this book, but with life, who deserve my gratitude and appreciation. Emily Haynes, my editor at Plume, who worked with my crazy schedule, extended deadlines, and was more understanding than she needed to be. And Jake Klisivitch for being my lucky #17—for after sixteen nos, he finally said YES, giving me the opportunity to become a published author. Andy Barzvi, my agent at ICM, who believed in me from the moment we spoke on the phone so long ago, and who is a true Tuff Chick, through and through. Emily, her assistant, who tracked me down all over the world to get this book done. Scott Simpson at APA, who believes in my present and my future. Russ, for teaching me so much about remodeling a home, and for teaching me that I can do it if I just try. Adam "Helfy" Helfman, who provided so much great information for the HAP portion of this book. Kate "Peppers" Costanzo and Laurin "Fluff" Coury, for keeping me sane. Dolf de Roos, for inspiring me to think greater than I ever thought possible and who continues to inspire me in both real estate and life. Randall Wallace, who inspires me to be a great writer just by listening to him chat about life. Sandy Fox, and everyone at Fox Law Group, for their hard work and belief in me. Mary Catherine Hamelin for being so much more than a photographer.

I want to thank Tom Forman, who created my show, who took a chance on me and gave me the opportunity of a lifetime. Denise Cramsey, my executive producer, who inspires me to be my best by simply being who she is—a strong leader and a true Tuff Chick who stands for honesty, loyalty, and a dedicated work ethic. To Vikki Dummer, Andrea Wong, David Goldberg, Lisa Higgins, Jenny Belcher, Rob Smith, and everyone at ABC and Endemol for giving me the unique opportunity to change families' lives week after week, and for being so supportive in all my endeavors. All of the cast and crew of *EM:HE* (my second family) for making the last few years the best of my life.

Thank you, Eric, for raising the bar, for remaining my best friend, and for checking off every box on my list. Just by being you, you challenge me to be the very best that I can be, and inspire me to achieve excellence.

And finally, I would like to thank all of the young Tuff Chix out there who come to the shows, who support me, and who write to me and let me know how you are living life to your fullest potential. You all are a true inspiration to me! Thank you!

Table of Contents

----

11. HANG IT UP

Reference

This is a schedule of everything you should do around the house each season, such as when it's a good time to clean your A/C filter, your rain gutters, etc.

INTRODUCTION

Let's Get Tuff!

Hello, ladies . . . and gentlemen. This is a book every woman needs around the house: a guide to easy home improvement and repairs that can save you hundreds, even thousands, of dollars. This is your guide to a better home and a better you. You are strong, independent, and Tuff!

WHAT TYPE ARE YOU?

There are two types of people out there: the DIY (do it yourself) type and the HAP (hire a professional) type. My goal is to turn you into the TC (Tuff Chix) type, one who fixes things or hires a professional because she *wants* to, not because she *has* to. This book will give you the knowledge you need to make that decision.

WHAT TO KNOW BEFORE YOU CALL A PRO

I'll give you the know-how and teach you the criteria to use to avoid getting ripped off. You will have the confidence to hire the right professional for each job and the knowledge to make informed inquiries before you hire.

YOU MAKE THE DECISION

EACH PROJECT WILL HAVE THE FOLLOWING INFORMATION:

 TUFF METER: From 1 to 10, with one being the easiest and 10 being the hardest, this meter will let you know what you are in for — and let you decide if you're up to the challenge.

 TIMER: This will give you an estimated time of how long it should take you to complete the project.

 TUFF TOOLS: This is a list of all the tools you will need to complete the project.

 SHOPPING LIST: An excuse to shop! This is a list of all the things you must purchase to complete the project. But don't forget about the tools list . . . you might want to look at that before you go shopping just in case you need to pick up a tool you don't already have. In most cases, I have listed a range. Please keep in mind that prices will vary according to your area.

 TOTAL PRICE: This is an estimate of the total cost of the materials needed to complete the project. Keep in mind that this is merely an estimate, and local prices may vary, but this will give you a good idea. In computing the total price, I have chosen the least expensive option in the range on the shopping list.

 HAP (Hire a Professional): This is an estimate of how much it would cost to hire a professional to do the same project. Use this to help you decide if it would be better to take on the project yourself, or use this as a price guide for hiring a professional if you decide to go in that direction. This way, you will know if you are getting ripped off. (This is also just an estimate. Prices will vary greatly per region.) Most professionals charge a minimum fee just to come to your house, so keep that in mind as well.

Review the project, and assess the Tuff Meter and the estimated time to complete the project. Then look at the alternative: how much it would cost to hire a professional to do it?

In some instances, you will want to tackle the project yourself. In others, it may be worth it to hire someone else, but if you do, at least you will know how much money you should be charged, how long it should take to complete the project, and how to get *exactly* what you paid (and asked) for.

Some subjects in this book will seem advanced, and some very elementary. The advanced projects (and some tools) will generally be something of a stretch and may not be in your comfort zone; however, I want you to be familiar with them. This book is about knowledge, and the more knowledge you have, the more power you have. I want you to be able to walk into any hardware store or onto any job site (which includes your own garage) and know what you are talking about.

My Story

Hi, everyone! If you choose to skip this section, I won't be offended, but I urge you to finish reading this paragraph. All you need to know is *don't be afraid*. You are tougher than you think, and you can successfully tackle every project in this book. You don't have to wait for someone else to do it, and you don't have to *pay* someone else to do it. You can do it yourself!

Don't be afraid to break a "nail." There was a time when I was intimidated and overwhelmed by things that needed fixing, yet didn't want to rely on someone else to fix them for me. Home improvement is not difficult; you just need know what to do. And even if you screw up, you can always fix your mistakes. My biggest hurdle was worrying too much. What if I did it wrong? What if I messed up? Well, guess what? You *can* mess up. I did! And you will too. I've learned so much by messing up, but the biggest thing I learned is that a mistake can always be fixed.

I remember learning how to put up drywall. It was in 1999, and I was dating a former construction worker (let's face it ladies, a buff man in a tool belt . . . yum). I was renting a two-bedroom house with two other girls. The home had a large dining room that we thought would be perfect as a third bedroom. I moved my belongings into the room and put up a folding screen, but soon realized I needed more privacy. We asked the owner if we could add double French doors to enclose it. She said yes, with one condition: that prehung French doors would fit in the opening exactly. We measured the opening and discovered that it was fourteen inches short of a perfect fit. What to do? I needed the privacy and this place was all we could afford, so moving was not an option. We *had* to make the doors fit. My crafty man had an idea: why not extend the wall by fourteen inches? I remember thinking that this was impossible, and that we'd never be able to do it ourselves. I was ready to throw in the towel, but with his reassurance, we went to the hardware store, purchased the materials, and got to work. Since I was *positive* this project could not be done, I wanted to be there every step of the way to witness the demise of his clever plan. We bought two-by-fours, drywall, screws, nails, drywall mud, and various other items that were so foreign to me at the time, they may as well have been creatures from another planet. At one point in the project, he handed me a shiny tool that looked something like a spatula with white toothpaste-type goop on it. My first inclination was to run the other way screaming, but instead he showed me how to apply the goop to the wall and how to smooth it out. I was *shocked*—it was so easy! I was drywalling! Yes, it took some finesse to get it smooth, but overall, it was simple. And the more times I tried, the better I became. Even when I messed up and left a big bump on the wall, it was easy to sand it down and start over. And talk about feeling empowered—I felt like I could do anything. I found myself spending every spare moment asking if I could help with his other projects. Soon I had learned the basics of drywalling, roofing, tiling, and framing.

With those limited skills under my tool belt, I felt like I could take on the world. Overdramatic? Maybe. But it felt good to know that I could make my own home improvements if I wanted to and no longer had to rely on someone else.

But that wasn't really the beginning. I'll have to take you back a few years to really show you how I became a Tuff Chick.

I have loved real estate since I was a little girl, although at the time, my real estate expertise was restricted to playing with dollhouses, building card houses, and touring model homes with my mom. When I was six, I had a life-size dollhouse in my bedroom. My mom tells the story of how I removed all the dolls from the dollhouse and began making furniture and redecorating. I also had a smaller scale dollhouse that I played with, and it too would receive regular makeovers. Anyway, at the time I was always more focused on the furniture and providing a comfortable environment for my cat than playing with any of the actual dolls.

Most people ask if I learned my craft from my father. Actually, my dad is a racecar driver, and although he can rebuild an engine with his eyes closed, I'm not sure he's ever picked up a hammer. And my mom? She is an excellent teacher, a whiz at investing, and simply an amazing person, but to her, fixing up the house meant keeping it spotless. My brother? Michael is one of my best friends, a professor, and a counselor who I would happily go to for personal advice, but definitely not for advice around the house.

I basically learned everything I know about home improvement on my own by picking up a little here and there over the years. To fill in the gaps (and there were many gaps), I bought how-to books. I bought book after book after book until I found sections that worked for me. Most of the books I found, however, were geared toward men who already knew about home improvement. They assumed that you had all the tools and knew all the terms to make it happen. Most of the books read like sleep-inducing manuals with no illustrations. I'm very visual, and I found it difficult to simply *read* directions—I needed to *see* the directions in action. And I desperately needed a "homegirl" dictionary. These books would throw out names of tools as if I was supposed to know what the heck they were talking about—and most of the time I had no idea. Even now, with years of experience, I still refer to some tools as "the sanding thingy" or "the fun-shape cutter outer" or "the corner edger." I feel it's perfectly fine if you don't know the official names—as long as you get the job done. I have written this book for all of you women (and men) who feel like I did. This is the book I wished I'd had during all those years when I was learning: one filled with descriptions, illustrations, a "homegirl" dictionary, and all you need to make you sound like you know what you are talking about at your local home-improvement store.

Okay, back to the life story. I attended Catholic school for twelve years, and then the University of California at Santa Barbara, where I studied psychology, theology, sunbathing, and beach living—all very important subjects. Throughout my school career, I loved learning, loved building businesses, and loved doing arts and crafts. (These will all come to be important later in the story.)

In 1994, my career took me out of the country. I worked in sales and marketing for four years, and after too many international flights and business dinners, I decided that was enough for me. I wanted to be successful and I wanted to have wealth. If traveling the world taught me anything, it was that most people either made their wealth (or held their wealth) in real estate. And since I wanted to own my own real estate, and still loved visiting model homes, I knew that real estate was the business for me. I decided that I'd better start making more money and saving it so that I could buy my first property and jump in the game.

In 2001, I became an apartment manager. My main motivation? Living for free. It did, however, serve another purpose: I could save money to buy my first property and learn about the real-estate business at the same time. I simultaneously started a wedding-coordinating business, and I worked from home while managing the apartments. It was an ideal situation. My goal was to save $25,000 my first year, buy a property, fix it up, and rent or sell it. In February 2002, a friend handed me a book that changed my life. It was called *Real Estate Riches*. When I say it changed my life, I mean it! I was so inspired by the teachings of Dolf de Roos and Robert Kiyosaki. I looked up to these great men and was inspired by the path they took throughout their lives, and how real estate shaped their futures. That book so motivated me that within four months I raised $250,000 from private investors to start my real-estate business. I purchased fourteen homes in three months. I soon realized, however, that although I had raised enough money to buy the homes, I had no money to hire someone to refurbish them. So, guess who did the work? Me—and whoever I could enlist to help me. I relied on all the books I had bought, to do everything from fix holes in walls to electrical rewiring and installing appliances. Fortunately, much of the work (like painting), was easy. I loved it! Well, I didn't love the actual physical labor, but I did love the feeling of accomplishment I got at the end of a project from knowing I had done it all. I was very proud of the work I did. Plus, the business was doing quite well. It was a rent-to-own program that helped people purchase their first homes. Not only was I making a more than sufficient income, I was helping people at the same time, which felt even better than the money in my pocket.

In the summer of 2003, I participated in a cable television show called *Monster House*. My motivation? To win free tools so I could fix up *more* homes. I appeared on the Christmas episode and went on my merry way with about four grand in new tools. I thought I had hit the jackpot. After the episode aired, I received a call from another show, *Extreme Makeover: Home Edition*. The casting agent, Andy, asked me to come down for an interview. Since the show had never aired, my question for him was, "Well, what do you win?" After a little chuckle, he explained that it didn't work like that.

I went to the interview and was promptly called back.

Since I had never really worked in television before, I didn't really know what a *callback* meant, except that I had to drive back down to Hollywood. I was told that I needed to construct something in front of them. They instructed me to bring all the materials and tools I would need, and said that I would be given one half hour to build something that would "wow" them—like a shelving unit or window box.

Well, since the thought of a shelving unit or window box didn't knock my socks off, I racked the old brain to come up with something clever. I decided to make a jack-in-the-box out of wood. I found an old toy at a secondhand store and took it apart to utilize the music apparatus. I replaced the creepy little clown head with a little house I had carved out of Styrofoam. I cut the *Extreme Makeover: Home Edition* logo out of Andy's business card and glued it to the little house. Since the new pine lid was much heavier than a plastic lid, I used parts from a rattrap for the spring. I cut a piece of the metal strap from my water heater to use as the clasp. I used the guts of the old toy for the music and latch release. I practiced three times before I headed down to Hollywood. When I arrived, I unloaded all my tools and materials and went to work. I finished in forty-two minutes and crossed my fingers as I cranked the little handle and the "da dee da dee da deedley dee" music played. I came to the "pop goes the weasel" point, and, to my excitement, my little house popped out successfully. Yippee! I gathered my things and left, wondering if they would ever call.

On my way out, I saw the next candidate—a strapping, muscle-packed carpenter with enough wood to construct a 4,000-square-foot home. I thought I was doomed. There was no way they'd pick me over this handsome devil. Days later, on my way to fix up one of my properties, Andy called with good news. He asked if he could send the contract over to "my people." Since I was "my people," I said sure, and gave him my personal fax number. I believed I was doing all of this for one episode, but as it turned out ABC sent over a six-year contract. Yeehaw!

I remember showing up for my first show, a little nervous, but very excited. Although I didn't know much about acting, I did know how to work, so I threw myself into the job. I remember calling my cousin Jaime, a cosmetologist in Illinois, while I painted into the night. I asked her to pack her bags and come out to California to help me. She nervously replied "I've never worked construction. I cut hair—not wood!" But what I knew about Jaime was that she is a hard worker and makes a mean scrapbook. "Home improvement is just big arts and crafts," I assured her. "We made things out of Popsicle sticks when we were little—this is the same concept, just on a bigger scale." With that persuasion, she hopped the next flight—and has assisted me on almost every show since. (If you watch closely, you can see her in the background of almost all of the shots in my workplace.) Ironically, Jaime went searching for proper work attire and encountered the same problem in the Midwest that I had here on the West Coast: *nothing for women*! In the two years prior to joining the show, I had searched for tool belts, work boots, work gloves, and home-improvement books designed for women. I searched and searched. At first, I thought I must be part of a very small minority of women in construction, which is not the case at all. I discovered that in America there are over one million registered women in construction, and that doesn't even include the weekend warriors who dabble a bit or women who fix up their home on a daily basis. It was then that we decided to create Tuff Chix, Inc., providing work wear, gear, and instructional assistance for women. Our motto was simple: "Who says girls can't be tough? (And why not be cute at the same time?)"

WHY THE PINK?

I had entered into a "man's" world when I entered construction, and although I typically looked like one of the guys while working on my own rental properties, I didn't want to look that way on national television. I wanted to stand out as a strong and capable woman displaying my skills. I decided to wear the least masculine color, which I figured was pink!

WHY THIS BOOK?

That brings us to today, and why you are reading this book. This book is designed for anyone who wants to improve their surroundings, in ways small or large. It's everything I wish I'd had when I started. It's the essential tool you need to create something great.

You don't have to read the book from cover to cover. Use it as your road map. This book is designed to make your life easier, save you a little money, and give you the tools you need to take care of yourself and your home.

Tuff Tips for Success

1. **Think big, start small:** Be realistic. Don't bite off more than you can chew. Divide larger projects into several

miniprojects. Identify your own limitations ahead of time to avoid frustration. Consider this: If you start and complete a small project, it will give you the encouragement and the self-confidence to tackle larger projects. On the other hand, if you start a project that is too big, you may get frustrated and abandon it, leaving you feeling unfulfilled and discouraged.

2. **Safety first:** Always be safe—even if you are fixing something "really quick." Wear the proper attire (nothing baggy), safety glasses, gloves, etc. Keep children and pets away from work areas. Follow safety instructions for the tools and materials you are using. Take your time and don't rush. Many accidents occur because of haste. Always keep a phone with emergency numbers handy in the event of an accident. And clean up as you go so that unneeded tools don't become the reason why you trip and fall.

3. **Ask questions:** Never be afraid to ask questions. If you find that you are dealing with someone who is snooty or not giving you the answers you seek, move on until you find someone who will. When I first started remodeling homes, I noticed that many customer-service people in hardware stores either did not think I was serious or gave me the "girl" answer. Some, I noticed, were just collecting a paycheck and really didn't know the answers to my questions. Instead of getting mad, I excused myself politely and kept asking my questions to other people until I received the answer I was after. Sometimes, it turned out that other customers were the most helpful.

4. **Be prepared:** Be sure you have all the materials and tools you will need. If you are going to disassemble something, take a picture or two for reference later when you need to put it back together again. Take a list to the hardware store. Nothing is more frustrating than going to the store, coming back and getting started,

and realizing that you forgot a few things and have to waste time going back again.

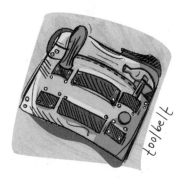

5. **Best tools:** When I invest in a good tool, regardless of whether I am buying or renting, it helps propel me toward success. I once sanded wood floors in my living room. They dated from 1939, were made of Douglas fir, and had been covered with wall-to-wall linoleum for decades, which left a thin, velvet-like covering stuck to the wood. I went to my local hardware store to rent a floor sander and was given the wrong one. After two weeks of sanding, I went back to the rental place and asked for a stronger machine. They finally allowed me to rent a belt sander, after I begged and persuaded them. They even made me sign a waiver, saying that I was likely to ruin my floors with such a strong tool. I took it home and was able to complete the project that night. If I had been given the proper sander at the beginning, it would have saved me time and the cost of a two-week rental.

6. **Measure twice, cut once:** *Always* measure twice, whether it's your first project or five-hundredth project. Not measuring properly is the main reason you hear curse words out on the job site.

7. **Don't cut corners:** There have been so many times when I've thought I could skip a step or hurry something along—and it just resulted in spending more time and more money. So follow instructions . . . *always!*

8. **Know your limitations and know when to stop:** When you are sleepy or exhausted, you are more apt to slip up and will more than likely make costly or even devastating mistakes that may even result in injury. Take breaks throughout the project to reenergize.

9. **Finish the job:** Don't give up. Do whatever you need to do to finish the job while your tools are still out (unless

you're tired, then please refer to number eight above). If you can't finish that night, finish first thing in the morning. Don't let a lot of time go by before you go back to the project. If you do, most likely the project will sit for months in its "almost done" state. Make the extra push to get it done!

10. **Use your number one tool—your brain:** Common sense is your best friend when fixing things around the home. Be smart every step of the way. If it feels wrong or unstable, it probably is. Listen to your intuition.

Getting to Know Your House

We are all capable of accomplishing anything we put our minds to. Part of the problem with home improvement stems from being unfamiliar with your home. Familiarity makes it easier to understand, and therefore, to conquer. So, let's go for a tour—take a few moments to examine your home, much like you would your outfit before going out on a date. Look around your house: Ever wonder what those pipes are for? Where they go? How about wiring? I want you to *know* your house, so if anything ever does go wrong, you will know exactly how to pinpoint the problem. Plus, a careful walk through your home will help prevent potential problems that may arise. Be observant, to prevent future catastrophes. Need help getting started? Take a look below.

As you go through this list, jot down things that need your attention or need a little repair.

Pipes There are many types of pipes in your own home. (See the pipe chart, pp. 194–195.) It's a good idea to inspect all the pipes in your home, whether located under sinks, under the house, or outdoors. Check for leaks by running your hand along them to see if they're moist and looking below them for puddles or slight discoloration.

Electrical Inspect all the outlets in your home. Remove the cover plates and look for any inconsistencies. Inspect all accessible exposed wiring to be sure it's in good shape. Look for frayed wires or small areas in the wiring that may have lost the plastic coating. Be sure all outlets located near sinks are protected with a GFCI (ground-fault circuit interrupter) switch. Locate your home's fuse box and familiarize yourself with the main switch and all the individual fuses. I think one of the most important things a person should know about her own home is where the fuse box is and how to reset a fuse once it's popped. It can be very frustrating when the power is out to be searching around with a candle or flashlight, unsure of where the main switch is. Locating it *before* there is a problem will help relieve stress when a problem does arise.

Electrical cords I intentionally made this heading separate from electrical wiring because it is so very important and is the cause of most household fires. Inspect *all* electrical cords, including those located behind the television, computer, stereo, lamps, and anything else you plug in. Most house fires occur because of loose or faulty wires. Check to make sure that each cord is in good shape—not chewed away by little critters or suffering from old age. Be sure that the circuit is not overloaded. This is most likely to occur around your television and stereo equipment, where it looks like a sea of tangled cords. (See "Fire Prevention," p. 225.)

Molding and baseboards Inspect all molding found near the floor and around doorjambs and window jambs. Make sure it is all in good shape (not rotting or loose). Note any spots that may need replacing or a new coat of paint.

Weather stripping Weather stripping is the lining, usually foam or rubber, around your doors that prevents drafts and leaks from entering your home. Check to make sure that it is not rotting, dry, cracked, or flaking and that it is securely in place. Even if it appears to be in good shape, it still may not be laid correctly. Here is a simple way to check for drafts. Wait until a windy day and hold a tissue up to the doorjamb. If the tissue moves, it's time to replace the weather stripping. This will also keep eight-legged creatures from obtaining easy access. That right there is my motivation for good weather stripping in my home—keeping spiders *out*! (See p. 112.)

Windows Inspect all windows, including sliding glass doors and small bathroom windows. Be sure each one closes and slides properly, that each lock is in working order to ensure safety, and that there is no draft coming through any part of the window or sill. This can save you hundreds of dollars a year on your heating and air-conditioning costs.

Fireplace Inspect your fireplace. If you've recently used your fireplace, remember that ashes can smolder for up to two weeks. You can clean up the ashes if you wear the proper safety equipment. Store the ashes in a covered steel container away from the house and away from any combustibles for about two weeks. That should give the ashes ample time to cool properly. Then simply throw them in the trash. Have your fireplace professionally inspected and cleaned annually. This will keep it free of debris and reduce the risk of unwanted fire.

Sinks Inspect all the sinks in your house, including kitchen, bathrooms, and laundry room. Look around the sink and the fixtures to ensure that everything is intact and securely fastened. Use your hand to feel around the perimeter of the sink, fixtures, and pipes to ensure that all are free of moisture. Check the water pressure. Is it too high or too low?

Gas and water mains Begin by locating your gas main and water mains. Label each main clearly. Familiarize yourself with how to shut off electrical, water, and fuel supplies to your home. This way, if you are ever in a situation where you must react quickly, you will know what to do. You can save the panicking for more important things.

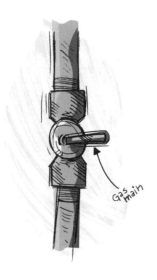

Gas main

Kitchen Take a moment to survey your kitchen. You may visit your kitchen every day, but I'm asking you to look at it in a different light. Inspect all of the countertop appliances, assuring that the cords are in good condition and that each appliance is working correctly. Locate the gas or electrical connection to the oven and/or stovetop. Be sure that those lines are in good shape. Inspect the refrigerator. Make sure that it has not accumulated excess dust around, above, or underneath it. Check your overhead ventilation systems to ensure that they are working correctly and are not clogged. Look at your lighting fixtures. Make sure all are clean and that each bulb is securely connected. Also, make sure the electrical outlet(s) near the sink are protected with a GFCI switch.

Flooring Walk through your home and inspect the flooring. Begin with the carpet. Is the pad still good? Are there any frayed, discolored, or worn areas in need of repair? Check where the carpet joins other flooring. This is an area where staples often begin to come through the carpet—a very painful step that can be avoided. Now look at the tile in your home. Are there any loose or broken tiles in need of repair? How does the grout look? Is it in need of cleaning or repair? Inspect vinyl flooring for areas that may be damaged or coming loose. This is a common problem with vinyl flooring in bathrooms and kitchens, especially around sinks, bathtubs, and toilets. Be sure to look for signs of mold on the floor. If you discover loose areas, these should be repaired immediately. This simple repair will prevent mold and decay in the future.

Ceilings Be careful not to get dizzy, but do take some time to look at *all* the ceilings in your home, including in bedrooms, hallways, bathrooms, entryways, living areas, dining room, laundry, garage, etc. Look for cracks or discoloration. If you discover any discoloration, it may be the sign of a bigger problem, such as water leakage somewhere in the roof or attic. You will need to investigate further to determine the source of the problem. For discoloration or stains on the ceiling, here's a quick tip: add bleach (and water) to a spray bottle and lightly mist the ceiling. This will take care of the stain, but you need to take care of the problem.

Phone jacks Inspect every phone jack in the house. Remember to look behind beds and appliances. Be sure to check for loose cover plates and any loose or exposed wires.

Bathroom Bathrooms are the busiest rooms in the house and can be the source of many problems. Leaks, moisture, and electrical cords can be a disastrous combination. Take a good look at each bathroom in your home. Be sure that sinks, fixtures, and pipes are clean and dry. Ensure that the flooring is in good shape. Check in corners or wet areas near the toilet and tub to see if it is peeling up. Make sure the shower curtain is in good shape and free of mold, and that the shower rod is secure and sturdy. If you have shower doors, make sure they are free of mildew and mold, and that they slide easily and are in good condition. Inspect your tub or tile enclosure to see that it is dry, with no mold or mildew buildup. Inspect the caulking. Is it in good condition? Is it moldy, dark, or peeling? Inspect the ventilation system. Is it clean and in good working order? Test the water pressure in all fixtures, including the sink and the tub or shower. Inspect the light switches and electrical outlets. Electrical outlets near a sink must be protected with a GFCI switch. Inspect the grout around the tile for discoloration and chipping. Double-check the cords on appliances. Are they in good working condition? Are you guilty of overloading a circuit (hair dryer, curling iron, flat iron, electric toothbrush, etc.) when getting ready? Inspect the light fixture to be sure it's clean, it's in good working condition, and that the bulbs are secure.

Bedroom You are in this room every day, but do you really take the time to notice possible hazards? Inspect the carpet, especially in the corners and where it meets other flooring. Is it worn or frayed? Is there any discoloration? This could be a sign of unwanted moisture. Check the electrical outlets and light switches. Do you have dimmer switches? Are they working properly? Check all electrical cords, including alarm clocks, lamps, television, stereo, etc. Check closet walls for discoloration, leaking, or moisture. Assure that the bar in the closet is sturdy and not overloaded. Make sure closet doors are hung correctly and slide properly. Check that you have a smoke detector in the room and that it is in good working order with a good battery. Do you have a ceiling fan? Make sure it works correctly and is clean. Ceiling fans can get off balance if they are not cleaned on a regular basis. Check to make sure that all pictures are stable and secure. Inspect your ceilings for cracks or discoloration.

Laundry room This room may seem squeaky clean to you, however, it is the site of most major flooding incidents and household fires, according to fire- and water-damage restoration companies. There are two main causes: supply lines and dryer ducts. Supply lines, which are little hoses that attach the water lines to the back of the washing machine (see p. 191). Look to make sure that the lines appear to be in good condition and are free of corrosion or rotting. Use your hand to make sure there are no pressure bubbles in the back of the hose and that it feels dry and free of corrosion. Allow me to explain why these supply lines are potentially dangerous. They are attached to water pipes that are on at all times, thus the water pressure is fierce and continuous. One line connects your washing machine to the hot water, and the other connects it to the cold water. If one of these supply lines should break, crack, or burst, water will not simply drip out—it will rush out. This typically happens while you are at work or on vacation. I've heard horror stories of people coming home to a foot of water, all because of one of these little babies. You would think something this important would be expensive and hard to switch out, right? On the contrary. Each hose is about twelve dollars and can be replaced in just a few minutes. Also, consider installing a pan underneath your washing machine to catch excess water. Check your dryer duct to ensure that it is free of lint or other combustible materials. Clean out the lint screen and areas surrounding your dryer often. Keep all storage areas neat, clean, and dry. Make sure that articles of clothing have not fallen behind the washing machine or dryer—they can be potential fire hazards.

Attic Although attic spaces may be small and kind of creepy, you must get up there and look around at least once a year. Check to make sure your insulation is in good condition and has not been displaced anywhere. Check for leaks or discoloration of the wood or roof. To be sure the venting is working, look through the vents and check for clogs. Bad ventilation in attics not only increases heating and air-conditioning costs, it can also lock in moisture, which may result in mold. Droppings or tears in boards and insulation may be a sign of little critters. If you have critters living in your attic, they too can cause mold—since they use the insulation for a toilet, and the moisture can remain there for months.

Basement Here's something we Californians don't typically have, which may explain our fascination with them. There are several potential hazards to be aware of with basements, and you should inspect your basement every couple of months. Does it feel damp? Feel and look around for wet spots. Check all pipes for leakage and corrosion. Refer to the pipe chart on pages 194–195 to learn what each pipe is for, so if anything does go wrong, you will know exactly how to pinpoint the problem and how to explain it to a professional. Check all electrical boxes and cords to assure that there are no loose or exposed wires and that they are secured or fastened to a wall or beam.

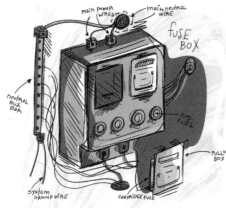

Fuse box This is an item with which I urge you to become familiar. Your fuse box is typically located just outside the house, near or in the garage, or in a back bedroom; however, they can be located anywhere. In a condo that I recently remodeled, the fuse box was in the kitchen. In my first apartment, it was behind the door in the guest room. It is a metal box that is usually 12 x 18 inches in size; however, they can range from as small as 5 x 7 inches to as large as 20 x 40 inches. Inspect the box and be sure it is clear of any wandering vines or plants that may have crawled up the wall. Trim nearby trees and brush so the area is always clear and the fuse box is accessible. You will save time and avoid headaches if you are familiar with the location of the fuse box, can access it easily, and have an understanding of each switch. Enlist the help of a friend who can stand inside the house and call out the exact areas that are turned off when you flip a switch. Be specific: It may not be just one room that is affected by any single switch. It could be the ceiling light in one room, an outlet in another, and yet another outlet down the hall. Once you have all the information written down, use masking tape and a permanent marker and label each switch. Yes, this may mean that you have to reset a few clocks, but I assure you it's worth it.

Let me share some stories of why this is so important. A friend of mine was complaining that her oven had stopped working. I asked her to check the fuse box. She found nothing unusual and told me the switch labeled "oven" appeared to be fine. She had bought the house just a year before and all the fuses were labeled. She ultimately called a repairman to inspect the oven, and after an hour and a half, they were both frustrated as to why it would not work. The repairman began checking every fuse and discovered that they were labeled incorrectly and the oven fuse had simply been flipped. He flipped it back and all was well in the world—except for her checkbook, which was now minus $150.

Halls and common areas Take a moment to inspect all the common areas in your home, including hallways and stairways. This is probably where you will find your air-conditioning unit. Open its doors and take a good look. Is it clean and free from dust? Remove the filter. Is it clean or in need of replacing? To keep your unit running efficiently, you should replace the filter every six months. Be sure that pictures and other wall hangings are securely hung and supported with a large enough nail or screw. Ensure you have smoke detectors and that they are in good working order with fresh batteries. Test smoke detectors by holding down the button until they beep. Inspect any staircase balusters or other railings you may have. Are they secure? Attempt to move the whole railing back and forth. Is it strong and stationary? Inspect each spindle. Are they in good condition and stationary? Check the air vents in your home. Are they clean and free of dust? Any dust on vents not only creates an environment for allergens, but also causes your air-conditioning unit to run less efficiently. Vents are very easy to clean, so don't put it off.

OVERALL PREVENTION

Now that you have familiarized yourself with your home's ins and outs, you are ready to maintain it. Turn to the reference section at back of this book and study the maintenance schedule. This will tell you exactly when to change filters, clean vents, check rain gutters, and what to do to keep your home in great condition. If you do not understand any of the items listed above, refer to the corresponding section in part 2 of this book and educate yourself further. A house can be your biggest burden or your greatest joy—you decide. Once you understand your home, you will be creating a safe haven for you and your family for years to come.

Permits

Before we get started, let's talk about laws—safety and prevention. Sure, not the most exciting topics, but very important nonetheless.

To abide with the laws and guidelines governing home improvement you often need to obtain permits. They do exactly what they sound like they might do—"permit" you to make a change to your home. Many projects, both large and small, require permits. Before you start any project, check with your local building department. Codes and requirements may differ from county to county. I'll list a few projects that definitely need permits, but there are hundreds more, so be sure to inquire. Always be sure that you (or any contractor you hire) acquire the proper permits. If you do not, you run the risk of faulty work or getting caught doing something you are not supposed to do. And you can't claim you just didn't know. I tried it—trust me, it doesn't work.

ME VS. PERMITS

I had the best of intentions. I was working on a remodel of a home built in 1939. I wasn't changing any of the outer floor plan, just fixing up the inside, replacing the windows, front door, and outdoor siding. I had removed the two sliding glass doors, reframed the two windows and front door, and just as I had both installed, a local, friendly inspector dropped by. He said it was the large trash bin in front of my house that tipped him off.

I promptly explained everything I was doing, with nothing to hide because I honestly only thought you needed permits if you changed the square footage of the home. I've learned a lot since then, to say the least. His eyes grew bigger and bigger as he started filling out some paperwork. He slapped me with a "stop order," insisting I cease all work until I acquired the proper permits. He explained to me that because I bought the house with some of the square footage not permitted, I had to make the necessary steps to permit those modifications, as well. "But I bought the house 'as is,'" I explained. He went on to explain that when I signed a disclosure that part of the property was not permitted, it became my responsibility, and I needed to rectify the situation.

This sent me into an eight-month uphill battle that required much more money than I imagined; plus, it left me without a front exterior wall through the entire process. Not only did I need a permit for the framing around the windows and doors, I now needed a permit for the new siding on the house, a soils report, a geological survey, a general survey of the house and the land, a plot plan, blueprints, "as-built" drawings, and countless other permits. Who knew? I was in the county office with tears streaming down my face. I couldn't believe that I was involved in a project where I had bitten off more than I could chew. I was mad at the inspector for stopping by, but more than that, I was mad at myself because I hadn't properly checked out the situation before I entered into it.

So heed my warning: do all the necessary research before you start! Permits cost anywhere from five dollars to thousands of dollars, depending on the scope of the work. Your local county office will have all the information you require. Go there first.

These projects (plus hundreds more) usually require permits:

- Decking
- Fencing
- Structural alterations
- New pool
- Finishing a basement
- Adding an electrical outlet or fixture
- Installing a water heater, fireplace, furnace, or AC unit

HAP: Hiring a Professional

What do you need to know before you hire a professional? Besides having a basic knowledge of the task at hand, which you will learn in this book, there are some questions you should always ask before you hire.

1. **Know:** Be *very* clear on what services you need, before you call. Many people think they need one thing, but once the professional gets there, he or she may recommend many other services. Be clear, and don't be oversold. Ask for *exactly* what you want to be accomplished.

2. **Quote:** Ask for a quote over the phone. Some professionals may not be comfortable giving an exact quote; if so, ask for a range. They will most likely want to make an appointment to give you a detailed quote. Always get a quote before any work is started.

3. **Permits:** Ask if the job requires permits from the city or county. Ask if they will provide these for you, or if you will need to get them yourself.

4. **Legal:** Ask for documentation from the company that it is insured and licensed to do the job. Make sure the license is up to date. Find out how long the company has been in business.

5. **References:** Ask for at least three references from recent clients, preferably some in your immediate area. Make sure they are *recent* references. Call these references and find out if the company is reliable, if the quality of the work was what was expected, and if they finished within the budget and on time.

6. **Better Business Bureau:** Check with the Better Business Bureau to see if there have been any complaints about the company. My mom was once fooled by a contractor that sent a salesman to give a quote for the job. The salesman was great—well dressed, well spoken, organized—and appeared trustworthy. The workers and owner, however, were quite the opposite. After the entire job turned out to be a disappointment, my mom called the bureau. Sure enough, there were several complaints similar to my mom's. If she had only made the call before, it would have saved her a lot of misery—and money.

7. **Contract:** Once a price is agreed upon, you have investigated references, and checked with the bureau, ask for a contract. The more specific it is, the better. That way there will be no confusion. This contract should include the following:

   a. **Dollar amount of the entire job:** Be clear if this amount includes materials.

   b. **Schedule of payments:** Typically, you will put a down payment of one-third. The remaining two-thirds of the payment can be at your discretion or

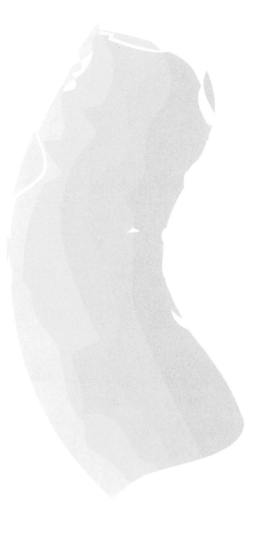

their recommendation. However, make sure that the final payment is to be made *after* the job is complete.

c. **Additional services:** If the job requires additional services or materials, they must notify you before proceeding.

d. **Work schedule:** When will the job begin? How often will they work on it? Every day? Weekdays only? What time will they be arriving in the morning, and what time will they complete work each day? How many workers will be present? Will they bring portable bathrooms or be using yours? Will they be eating there or going away for lunch?

e. **Completion date:** What date will the project be completed? If it is not completed at this time, what are the repercussions? Have you heard of the projects that are supposed to take "two weeks" and end up taking months? If there are no penalties for going over the promised time, a contractor most likely will. You can impose penalties per day that they go over schedule, as long as it is in the contract from the beginning.

f. **Contact:** Who will be your day-to-day contact? Is there a foreman or a lead carpenter? You want to make sure that you have one central person who you can rely on to listen to your questions and give reliable answers.

g. **Cleaning:** At the end of each day and at the end of the project, make sure they leave the premises clean. If this is not in the contract, they can just leave you with the mess. Although it is annoying and unprofessional, it is not against the law to leave a work site messy.

Now that you are aimed and ready, you can take on some projects!

PROJECTS

1

FIXING THE LITTLE BROKEN THINGS

There are potentially hundreds of little problems inside a house, condo, apartment, or wherever we reside. Ever think some of them seem too small to call someone in for repairs, or that some are so big that you just don't want to pay someone else to do them? Well, this section is for you. With a little knowledge, you can fix anything—and everything—around your house.

Cement and Concrete

REPAIRING A MINOR CRACK IN CONCRETE

Even if the crack is small, it is important to repair it. Tiny cracks left in concrete can lead to bigger cracks because water, moisture, and frost can creep inside.

> **SAFETY:** Although it looks like a harmless material, concrete is VERY DANGEROUS! It's high in alkaline, which means it can act like acid and burn right through your skin. Always wear safety glasses, gloves, a long-sleeved shirt, and long pants while working with concrete.

TUFF METER: 2

TIMER: 10 minutes (with 2 hours to dry)

TUFF TOOLS: Trowel

SHOPPING LIST: Cement caulk (make sure it is expandable and flexible; $6.99/tube)

TOTAL PRICE: $6.99

$75

What is concrete? Concrete is the basic building block of construction. It is versatile and easy to use. It can be useful, providing walkways or stairs. It can be powerful, holding up giant structures such as buildings, homes, and freeways. And it can be beautiful, bringing style and elegant touches to modern homes as floors and kitchen countertops.

Although they may seem interchangeable, the terms cement *and* concrete *actually have different meanings. Cement is the component that hardens masonry mixtures when water is added. It is a combination of lime, silica, alumina, iron, and gypsum. Concrete is a mixture of cement, gravel, and sand. Around the home, however, people tend to use these terms interchangeably.*

How to repair a minor crack in concrete:

1. Clean the area so that it is free of debris. You can sweep it out, or use a wire brush or vacuum it out with a shop vac. It must be dry before you move to step 2.

2. Apply caulk into crack. Use an ample amount of caulk to fill the crack to just above the surrounding surface.

3. Take a trowel and smooth out the caulk so that it is level with the surrounding area. If the crack is small enough, you can use your finger to smooth out the caulk (make sure to wear a rubber glove).

4. Let dry for at least two hours.

FILLING A GAP IN CONCRETE

Gaps are like cracks, only bigger. Gaps between concrete surfaces and structures can create moisture problems, yet they are overlooked in most homes. Gaps are easy to fill, and doing so will keep the foundation of your home dry.

TUFF METER: 2

 TIMER: 20 minutes (with 4 hours to dry)

 TUFF TOOLS: Trowel (or oil-rubbed spoon)

 SHOPPING LIST: Cement caulk (make sure it is expandable and flexible; $6.99/tube)

TOTAL PRICE: $6.99 $75–$150 for a minor crack

How to fill a gap in concrete:

1. Make sure the area is dry and clear of debris.

2. Take caulking and apply it to the entire length of the gap. Use generously.

3. You can even out the caulking with a glove-covered finger, a trowel, or the back of a spoon rubbed with oil. You can use *any* oil—baby, vegetable, olive, even suntan oil.

4. Let dry for at least 4 hours.

REPAIRING A SMALL HOLE IN CONCRETE

How to repair a small hole in concrete:

1. Break away any loose or unstable material. The easiest way to do this is with a small chisel and hammer.

2. Clean up any excess debris. If you can use a shop vac, it's best. Make sure area is dry.

3. Use a paintbrush to apply the bonding adhesive to the entire area that needs to be patched.

 TIMER: 20 minutes for each step (with 2 hours to dry between steps)

 TUFF TOOLS: Chisel, hammer, paintbrush, trowel

 SHOPPING LIST: Reinforced cement patching compound ($13.50/gallon)

 TOTAL PRICE: $13.50 **$100**

4. Fill the area with the reinforced patching compound, only adding about ½ inch at a time.

5. Wait about 30 minutes for the layer to dry.

6. Apply additional layers until you have filled the hole to just above the surrounding surface area.

7. Use a trowel to smooth out the area being repaired, until it is level with the surrounding area. It's okay to let the mixture feather over the surrounding area to get a good, level base.

8. Allow the mixture to cure (or dry). Although it will take months to completely cure, you will begin to see hardening within the first few minutes, and it will be hard enough to walk on within 2 hours.

TUFF CHIX DICTIONARY

Plaster is a mixture of lime, sand, and water that is applied as a liquid paste to ceilings and internal walls of a building and that dries to a smooth hard surface. You will find this material on outside walls of homes, as well. Typically, internal walls are either drywall or lath and plaster. Before you attempt to patch a hole or crack, determine which type of wall you are dealing with.

Plaster Repair
CRACKS IN PLASTER

TUFF METER: 8

TIMER: 45 minutes (with 2 hours to dry between coats)

TUFF TOOLS: Wide drywall knife, washcloth

SHOPPING LIST: Fiberglass tape ($12–$37), joint compound ($4.95), sandpaper (100 grit; $1.89/6 sheets)

TOTAL PRICE: $18.84

$25/hour of labor ≈ $200 (est., depending on how large the job)

How to repair a crack in plaster:

1. If the crack is large, the first thing you want to do is make it bigger. What? Isn't that more work? No, trust me. You want to extend your work area to make the repair last. If you just fill in the crack, it will come right back. Make the crack larger with a utility knife.

2. Then clean the area around the crack. Scrape off any loose plaster or wall texture around the crack. Apply a thin coat of joint compound in the crack, letting it feather out over the crack.

fiberglass mesh tape

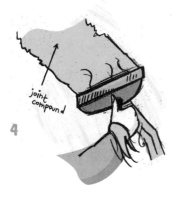

joint compound

3. Take fiberglass tape and cover the entire crack. This tape allows for mobility so that future cracks can be avoided.

4. Apply a thin coat of joint compound with a wide dry-wall knife, much like you would frost a cake, until the tape is completely covered and smooth.

5. Allow a couple of hours to dry.

6. Take fine sandpaper and smooth out the compound when completely dry.

7. Apply as many coats as necessary to assure that the crack and tape are completely covered and appear to be smooth and flush with the wall. Allow each coat to dry properly.

8. Try to recreate the texture of the wall. Do this by putting a small amount of joint compound on a wet washcloth. Dab it onto the wall like you would a sponge, until you have closely matched the surrounding texture, adding or subtracting wherever necessary. If you have a smooth wall, just leave it smooth.

9. You are ready to prime. Make sure you use a primer before you paint because the new substance on the wall is much more porous and will absorb paint more quickly, changing the color and texture of the paint slightly.

10. Allow two coats of primer to dry before applying the paint to match the wall.

HOLES IN PLASTER

How to repair a hole in plaster:

1. Smooth out the edges of the hole with a utility knife.

2. Clean all debris from area. Make sure area is dry.

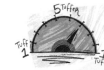

TIMER: 1 hour (with 2 hours to dry)

TUFF TOOLS: Wide drywall knife, washcloth

SHOPPING LIST: Concrete bonding agent ($17/gallon), wire mesh ($0.20/sq. ft.), drywall screws ($3.99/lb. for 2-inch screws), fiberglass mesh tape ($12–$37), sandpaper (100 grit; $1.89/6 sheets)

TOTAL PRICE: $35.08

$35–$40/hour
≈ $200 (est.)

3. Brush concrete bonding agent onto the wood (lath) and old plaster surrounding the hole.

4. Attach wire mesh to the existing wood (lath) with drywall screws. Why? Because, like the tape when you are fixing cracks, the wire mesh creates a surface that the joint compound can adhere to.

Bonding Agent

3

5. Fill in the hole with joint compound and smooth the outermost portion with a wide drywall knife to just below the surface of the surrounding area.

6. Where the compound meets the old edge, apply fiberglass mesh tape. You will basically be making a square box around a round hole.

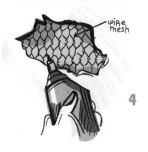

wire mesh

4

Fiberglass mesh tape

6

7

7. Apply a thin coat of joint compound with a wide drywall knife, much like you would frost a cake.

8. Allow a couple of hours to dry.

9. Apply as many coats as necessary to assure that the hole and tape are completely covered and appear to be smooth and flush with the wall. Allow each coat to dry properly.

10. Take 100-grit or similar sandpaper and sand over the joint compound until smooth.

11. Try to re-create the texture of the wall. Do this by putting a small amount of joint compound on a wet washcloth. Dab it onto the wall like you would a sponge, until you have closely matched the surrounding texture, adding or subtracting wherever necessary.

12. You are ready to prime. Make sure you use a primer before you paint because the new substance on the wall is much more porous and will absorb paint more quickly, changing the color and texture of the paint slightly.

13. Allow two coats of primer to dry before applying the paint to match the wall.

> **SAFETY:** Wear safety goggles and gloves. Unlike concrete, joint compound and drywall are not toxic, but you should protect your skin and eyes anyway.

Drywall Repair

Drywall is also sometimes called wallboard, Sheetrock, gypsum, or plasterboard. Cracks in drywall are commonly found where two sheets meet up or where the tops of walls meet the ceiling. They typically occur over time as a house settles. There are many quick ways to patch a crack, but you should

TUFF CHIX DICTIONARY

Drywall is a flat four-by-eight-foot sheet of reinforced plaster made of gypsum sandwiched and enclosed by several layers of sturdy paper. It is used mainly for interior walls and ceilings. In building a house, drywall is fastened against the wooden framing.

never cut corners in this area, because they will always come back to haunt you.

It is easy to damage drywall in everyday life: bumps from kids (and adults), moving furniture, or a doorknob that opens a bit too far. But the best part about drywall is that it is easy to repair. You just need to know the simple steps of how to do it.

CRACKS IN DRYWALL

TUFF METER: 6

TIMER: 45 minutes (with 2 hours to dry between each coat)

TUFF TOOLS: Wide drywall knife, washcloth

SHOPPING LIST: Joint (or "setting") compound (mud; $4.95/tub), joint tape ($1.78/250 feet), sandpaper (100 grit; $1.89/6 sheets)

TOTAL PRICE: $8.62
$25/hour
≈ $150

How to repair a crack in drywall:

1. Apply joint compound inside the crack using a wide drywall knife. Use ample amounts to fill the crack and create an even surface with the surrounding area. Allow time to dry. You can tell when it is dry by waiting until it turns an even, white color. If it is still a shade darker in some areas, it is not completely dry. This usually takes a couple of hours. To speed up the process, you can add heat or a fan to the area.

2. Sand this area with 100-grit or similar sandpaper, or a damp washcloth, for a smooth surface. This does not

have to be perfect, however, since this is just the bottom layer.

3. Apply additional joint compound (mud) to the crack.

4. Immediately apply paper joint tape over the entire crack in the wet mud.

5. Smooth the joint tape with the wide drywall knife, working from the center outward.

6. Use additional joint compound to apply layers over the tape and blend (feather) it into the surrounding areas.

7. Let dry for several hours.

8. Repeat these steps until the repaired area blends with the surrounding wall. Don't worry—if you mess up, you can always sand it down and start over.

9. Sand with 100-grit or similar sandpaper until smooth.

10. Try to re-create the texture of the wall. Do this by putting a small amount of joint compound on a wet washcloth. Dab it onto the wall like you would a sponge, until you have closely matched the surrounding texture, adding or subtracting wherever necessary.

11. You are ready to prime. Make sure you use a primer before you paint because the new substance on the wall is much more porous and will absorb paint more quickly, changing the color and texture of the paint slightly.

12. Allow two coats of primer to dry before applying the paint to match your wall.

A SMALL HOLE IN DRYWALL

How to repair a small hole in drywall:

If it is a small enough hole (about the size of a golf ball or smaller) with no cracks or damage around the edge, simply follow the instructions for cracks in drywall (see p. 41).

A BIGGER HOLE IN DRYWALL

TUFF METER: 7

TIMER: 45 minutes (with 2 hours to dry)

TUFF TOOLS: Wide drywall knife, washcloth

SHOPPING LIST: "Peel and stick repair patch" ($3.79–$6.89) **or drywall patching kit or joint compound (mud; $4.95) and sandpaper (100 grit; $1.89/6 sheets)**

TOTAL PRICE: $5.68

$25/hour
≈ $75 (est.)

How to repair a bigger hole in drywall:

1. If the hole is bigger (anything larger than the golf ball but smaller than a softball) or has cracked edges, you need to do a little bit more. Get a "peel and stick repair patch" from the hardware store.

2. Peel and stick the patch over the hole.

3. Apply a thin layer of joint compound over the entire patch with a wide drywall knife.

4. Let the compound dry.

5. Add a second or third coat until the area blends in with the surrounding areas.

6. Let the compound dry and the patch set until everything is completely dry.

7. Sand with 100-grit or similar sandpaper until smooth.

3

8. Try to re-create the texture of the wall. Do this by putting a small amount of joint compound on a wet washcloth. Dab it onto the wall like you would a sponge, until you have closely matched the surrounding texture, adding or subtracting wherever necessary.

9. You are ready to prime. Make sure you use a primer before you paint because the new substance on the wall is much more porous and will absorb paint more quickly, changing the color and texture of the paint slightly.

10. Allow two coats of primer to dry before applying the paint to match your wall.

A LARGE HOLE IN DRYWALL

TUFF METER: 8

TIMER: 1 hour (with 2 hours to dry)

TUFF TOOLS: Wide drywall knife, washcloth, utility blade or drywall saw

SHOPPING LIST: Joint compound (mud; $4.95), drywall screws ($3.99/pound for 2-inch screws), fiberglass mesh tape ($12–$37) or joint tape ($1.78/250 feet), sandpaper (100 grit; $1.89/6 sheets)

TOTAL PRICE: $24.61

$30–$50/hour ≈ $150 (est.)

If your hole is larger than a softball, the job becomes a little bit more intense but something you can handle, nonetheless.

How to repair a large hole in drywall:

1. Square the hole by cutting around it in a square pattern using a utility blade or drywall saw.

2. If the hole is near a stud, you are in luck. Cut the drywall back to about ½ inch over the stud and skip to step 7.

3. If there is no stud, you will have to make your own tiny studs.

4. Take small pieces of scrap wood or drywall and place them behind the drywall surface.

5. While holding them close, use drywall screws to attach these tiny studs to the outmost edges of your new square hole. These are what you will use to attach your new piece of drywall.

6. Cut the drywall patch a little bit smaller than your square hole so it will fit easily into the hole.

7. Attach the patch to the tiny studs or main studs in all four corners with drywall screws.

fiberglass mesh tape

8. Apply fiberglass mesh tape to all the seams.

9. Apply a thin layer of joint compound over the entire patch with a wide drywall knife.

10. Let the compound dry.

11. Add a second or third coat until the area blends in with the surrounding areas.

12. Let the compound dry and patch set until everything is completely dry.

13. Sand with 100-grit or similar sandpaper until smooth.

14. Try to re-create the texture of the wall. Do this by putting a small amount of joint compound on a wet washcloth. Dab it onto the wall like you would a sponge, until you

have closely matched the surrounding texture, adding or subtracting wherever necessary.

15. You are ready to prime. Make sure you use a primer before you paint because the new substance on the wall is much more porous and will absorb paint more quickly, changing the color and texture of the paint slightly.

16. Allow two coats of primer to dry before applying the paint to match your wall.

Tuff Tips

- Use fast-setting joint compound if you want to finish a project in one day.
- Instead of using sandpaper that creates dust, take a damp sponge or washcloth and scrub the area.

Ceramic Tile

TUFF CHIX DICTIONARY

Ceramic is porcelain made essentially from a clay mineral fired at a high temperature. Ceramic tile is the term commonly used to refer to most of the tile you will find in homes.

Grout is a cement-based powder that is mixed with water. Some grout is mixed with other additives that make it harder for water to penetrate. Grout fills the area between tiles not only to give it a nice, finished look, but also to create a watertight seal. There are two types of grout out there: sanded and nonsanded. Nonsanded grout is usually used for smaller gaps (about $\frac{1}{8}$-inch or smaller) and typically with smoother tiles such as polished marble and porcelain. Sanded grout is usually used for wider gaps and can be used with most manufactured tile and natural stone.

DISCOLORED GROUT

If your grout is discolored, you may not have to replace it. It might be as simple as bleaching it.

TUFF METER: 1

TIMER: 1 hour, including a 30-minute break

TUFF TOOLS: Spray bottle and a stiff brush or toothbrush

SHOPPING LIST: Liquid bleach ($4.99/gallon)

TOTAL PRICE: $4.99

$15/hour
≈ $50 (est.)

How to clean discolored grout:

1. Get a spray bottle and fill it with 2 parts water to 1 part bleach.

2. Spray generously over the grout, making sure not to spray it on anything the bleach might stain.

3. Let the bleach mixture sit for 30 minutes.

4. Use a small stiff brush or toothbrush to scrub the grout.

5. Rinse off, or use a sponge to clear the bleach from the grout.

6. If the discoloration still persists, repeat all steps. If the grout is stained beyond cleaning, you may want to replace it.

> **SAFETY:** When working with grout and tile, be sure to wear safety goggles, a dust mask, and gloves.

Tuff Tip

When using grout, follow the directions on the back of the box or bag. Make sure you mix it to a toothpastelike consistency.

REPLACING GROUT

If you have a section of grout that is missing, chipped, broken, or discolored beyond cleaning, you can repair and replace it.

TUFF METER: 4

TIMER: 2 hours

TUFF TOOLS: Chisel or small putty knife and small hammer, or utility knife, float, vacuum or shop vac

SHOPPING LIST: Small bag or box of grout ($9.97/gallon), grout sealer ($7.97/pint)

TOTAL PRICE: $17.94

$15–$20/hour
≈ $50 (est.)

How to replace grout:

1. Scrape out the existing grout with a chisel or small putty knife and a small hammer, or simply a utility knife. Be careful not to tap too hard and chip the surrounding tile.

2. Clean the area with a vacuum to remove excess sand, dust, and debris.

3. Run your hand over the grout. Does is feel smooth or a little rough? If it's smooth, you will need to buy unsanded grout. If it is a little rough, you will need to buy sanded grout. Take a piece of the grout with you to the hardware store to match the color. You only need to buy a small bag or box of grout for small repair jobs. Buy the smallest one you can find.

4. Mix up the grout according to the directions on the back of the bag or box.

5. Take your float, load it with grout and spread grout over the repair area, making sure to push it down into the gap.

6. Scrape away all excess grout by holding your float on its side or at an angle, making sure the grout is smooth and even, just at or slightly below the tile surface.

7. Let the grout dry (or "set up"). This should take about 2 hours.

8. Remove all excess grout and messiness with a damp sponge. Rinse out the sponge frequently and keep it clean. The water will appear chalky or cloudy until it is clean.

9. After grouting, do not get the surface wet for at least 24 hours.

10. After the grout has set up for 1 week, it should be completely cured. Now it is time to apply a grout sealer. You can buy this at your local hardware store and should follow the directions that come with the product.

REPLACING BROKEN TILE

How to replace a broken tile:

1. Scrape out grout with a chisel or small putty knife and a small hammer, or simply a utility knife.

2. Break the tile in need of repair into tiny pieces using the small hammer.

3. Remove all the pieces of the broken tile. Use a utility knife or small putty knife to

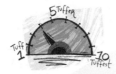

TIMER: 1 hour; grout: 20 minutes

TUFF TOOLS: Chisel or small putty knife and small hammer, or utility knife, float, vacuum or shop vac

SHOPPING LIST: Tile adhesive ($1.49/5.5 ounces), small bag or box of grout ($9.97/gallon), blue painter's tape ($5.59)

TOTAL PRICE: $17.05

$18/sq. ft. or $20–$30/hour ≈ $150 (est.)

5

6

scrape the area clean of all excess debris. There will probably be quite a bit of debris left from under the tile, so scrape well! Vacuum the area to remove small particles.

4. Test fit the new tile in the opening. It should have an equal gap on all sides and must also sit flush to the surrounding surfaces.

5. Apply adhesive to the back of the tile and immediately place it into the area being repaired. Use even force with both hands, slightly twisting the tile until it is level with the surrounding area. You want to make sure that the adhesive does not push up the tile unnecessarily.

6. Use a piece of blue painter's tape (a type of masking tape) to the tile to hold it in place for 24 hours.

7. Remove the tape and clean around the replaced tile again to assure no debris, dust, or particles have accumulated in the gaps. Clean if necessary.

8. Grout around the tile, following steps 3–10 in the previous project.

TUFF METER: 4

TIMER: Cleaning/removing: 25 minutes; caulking: 20 minutes

TUFF TOOLS: Utility knife, small putty knife, scrub brush

SHOPPING LIST: Bleach ($4.99), caulking ($2.99–$9.99/tube)

TOTAL PRICE: $7.98

$10–$15/hour ≈ $50 (est.)

Take a moment to inspect your tub, shower stall, and anywhere else you might have caulking. Is it in good shape or does it need replacing? If water gathers in that area, the caulk may be full of mold or mildew, or may be separating from its intended place. This is an easy fix. As long as you have the right materials, you can remedy this problem in a snap.

How often should you replace caulking? Depending on its type, caulking can last anywhere from one to forty years. However, if it's in a place that gets a lot of moisture, you may need to replace it every couple of years. It's best to just take a look. When it looks bad, replace it.

> **SAFETY:** Caulking is usually biodegradable and nontoxic and will wash off hands or clothing when it's still wet. Once it hardens, it is easy to scrape off. I use rubber gloves when caulking to keep my fingers clean, but you don't need to.

TUFF CHIX DICTIONARY

The verb to caulk, *Webster's* tells me, means, *"to stop up and make tight against leakage." Caulk (or caulking) is a clear or white substance used to do just that—stop up and avoid leakage. It has the consistency of toothpaste when it comes out of the tube and sets up to a hard, yet rubbery, consistency, making it a great sealant for cracks, joints, and seams.*

How to recaulk a tub or shower stall:

1. First, remove the damaged caulking with a utility knife by cutting at the very edge where the caulking meets the surface. Then pull it away with your hand. Remove any excess by scraping with the utility knife or small putty knife.

2. Clean the area well. Use a little bit of bleach and a scrub brush. This will prevent mildew and mold from coming back quickly.

3. Dry the area thoroughly. Let it dry for at least a couple of hours before you begin.

4. You will apply the caulk directly out of the container or caulking gun. Start by cutting off the tip of the tube after you take off the cap. Cut off just a little. There should be a mark on the tube itself, but just in case there is not, only cut off a little less than ¼ inch. Apply the caulk directly to the replacement area as a thick bead (or line), starting in the corner or at one end. Squeeze the tube slowly so that you leave an even, solid line behind you as you go.

5. Once you have a line of caulk along the replacement area, run your finger (wet it first so it doesn't stick) along the bead, which will even out the caulking. You

Tuff Tip

When you go to buy caulking, make sure that you don't skimp. Spend the couple of extra dollars and purchase a good caulking. It will last longer and provide a better moisture barrier.

can also do this with a caulking tool, but I say save the money and use what God gave you.

6. Take a clean finger or paper towel and wipe up any excess caulk, including any that may have blended out too far.

7. Let it dry for 24–48 hours before using the tub or shower.

Patching Wallpaper and Removing Bubbles

Most bubbles you see in wallpaper are just air pockets. But sometimes, a bit of debris causes the pocket. In order to tell the difference, press on the area and see if you feel anything. If you do, cut a small X on the wallpaper with a utility knife, remove the debris, apply a little adhesive to the back of the wallpaper, and press it back against the wall. Smooth out any ripples.

If the bubble is an air pocket, simply slice the wallpaper carefully. If the wallpaper has a pattern, try to cut along the pattern to conceal your work. Apply adhesive to the back of the wallpaper and gently push it back onto wall. Remove any excess adhesive and use your hands to smooth out the paper.

Tub Tip

In order to be sure that your caulking won't crack or stretch unnecessarily, fill the tub with water before you caulk, making sure that you don't splash any water up into the caulking area. Caulk with the tub full. The water will provide the necessary weight to position the tub where it settles when you use it on a daily basis. Leave the tub full of water until the caulking is completely dry (twenty-four to forty-eight hours).

TUFF METER: 3

TIMER: 1 hour

TUFF TOOLS: Scissors, utility knife, small putty knife, damp washcloth, remnant of wallpaper, ruler, removable tape

SHOPPING LIST: Wallpaper adhesive ($3.64/quart)

TOTAL PRICE: $3.64

$25/hour

1

2

How to patch wallpaper:

1. Find a remnant of wallpaper that matches the piece that needs to be replaced. Cut a section that is slightly larger than the damaged area. Apply it to the wall over the damaged area with removable tape. Make sure the pattern lines up.

2. Take your utility knife and cut through both the wallpaper patch and the wallpaper that is on the wall. This will ensure that you have a replacement piece the exact same size as your opening.

3. Remove your patch and wet the damaged area. Gently peel the damaged piece away, being careful not to damage the surrounding areas. Scrape away any excess glue or wallpaper in the area. You may need to use a hot, wet washcloth to ease the glue off the wall. Make sure the wall is clean and dry before you continue.

4. Apply adhesive to the back of the patch and carefully place it in the clean, dry area. Make sure the pattern matches up.

5. Smooth out the patch with your hand or a ruler, making sure there are no bubbles.

6. Wipe away any adhesive that might have oozed out with a damp washcloth. Let dry.

TUFF METER: 4

TIMER: Depends on what you find. I'd leave a weekend for this project.

TUFF TOOLS: Metal scraper

SHOPPING LIST: Squirt bottle ($3), sandpaper ($1.89/6 sheets)

TOTAL PRICE: $4.89   **$25/hour**

How to remove wallpaper:

The Tuff Meter will vary on this project. I have removed wallpaper that has been really simple and took no time at all. I remember, however, trying to remove the 1970s detailed velvet wallpaper from my mom's bathroom. It took me *days* and made me want to scream. I also learned a lot, however, from that project, so perhaps my time was not wasted.

I learned that the best way to remove difficult wallpaper is good ol' warm water. I've tried it all—the wallpaper steamer, the chemicals, the soap and water combination—nothing worked, and it all cost me money and time. So take it from me: when you are ready to remove wallpaper, invest in a good squirt bottle and have some hot water standing by.

1. Every good job starts with preparation. For this prep, simply move all furniture away from the wall and cover it with drop cloths. If you are in a bathroom with a tile floor, you are pretty much ready to go.

2. Begin in the corners. See if you can grab a piece of wallpaper and begin to pull. Sometimes you will hit the jackpot and it will simply peel right off. Most times, you will be able to pull some off with ease, but you will be left with some stubborn spots of paper and a lot of leftover glue residue.

3. Remove all that you can while dry.

4. Fill your squirt bottle with hot water. It just has to be hot/warm (*not* boiling). Out of your tap is fine.

5. Spray a good mist on the wall, starting at the top and moving in about a four-foot section across. Be sure to mist well.

6. Repeat about four times, until the wall is saturated. Be careful, however, not to *over*saturate, as it can ruin drywall if it gets too wet.

7. Take your scraper and *gently* start scraping away wallpaper and/or glue residue. I say "gently" because it is *very* easy to nick or gouge the wet drywall.

8. Repeat this process until the entire wall is wallpaper/glue free.

9. Some places will tell you to score the wallpaper with a razor blade, but this is never a good idea. This will leave your wall scratched and nicked.

10. If you are still left with residue on the wall, grab some sandpaper and sand it away. You can start with a really rough surface (60 grit), and gradually work your way up to a very smooth surface (220 grit). This should remove all gunk from the wall. Keep in mind that you may have to go through a lot of sandpaper, as it will get "gunked up" with all the glue.

2

PAINTING

Painting is easy and an inexpensive way to change the look of a room, especially if the walls and ceilings are already in good shape, and you just want to change the color. In this chapter we'll discuss painting inside the home. For the exterior, see the "Outdoor" chapter.

Types of Paint

There are two main kinds of paint: water-based latex paint and oil-based (or alkyd-based) paint. My favorite kind is latex. Why? Because it's easy to clean up with soap and water, it's easy to clean and rinse the brushes, and it dries faster. Many professional painters, however, like the oil-based paints. They say that they go on smoother and are more forgiving since they take longer to dry. They are a good option if you are planning to do detailed faux-finishing work, but I've even used latex for that application as well. Also, sometimes there are local building codes and restrictions about using oil-based paints, so check with your local building inspector before using them.

Paints also come in a variety of finishes, ranging from flat to high gloss. For a detailed list of paint finishes, see the chart on pages 62–63.

> **SAFETY:** Wear goggles, gloves, and long-sleeved clothing. Some paints are toxic, while others are water-soluble. It is always best, however, to wear gloves and cover your body with some old clothes that you don't mind getting soiled. Especially when using a roller, it is important to wear safety goggles, since specs of paint tend to spray off the roller and can hurt your eyes. If paint does get into your eyes, immediately rinse them with water.

TUFF CHIX DICTIONARY

Although I think everyone pretty much knows what paint is, I thought I would once again share Webster's *definition. Paint is "a mixture of a pigment and a suitable liquid to form a closely adherent coating when spread on a surface in a thin coat."*

PAINT CHART: TYPES OF PAINT

TYPE OF PAINT	DEFINITION	USES	PROS	CONS
Oil Based/Enamel	Pigment mixed with an oil base.	Walls	Slow drying, so good to use for faux painting. Long lasting and more resistant to fading. Once on a wall, easy to keep clean. Works well on rough services.	Slow drying, hard to clean up or dilute. Must use paint thinner or turpentine. They are usually more expensive. More difficult to use.
Water-based/Latex	Pigment mixed with a water and latex base.	Walls	Dries quickly. Easy to clean up, easy to wash (and reuse) brushes. Easy to use. Less expensive than oil-based.	Perhaps only that it is quick drying, so not good for faux uses.
Wood Stain	Very thin type of paint that penetrates the surface (instead of typical paint that stays on top of the surface). It contains pigment.	Wood	Enhances wood, doesn't cover wood.	If you want to cover the wood completely, this won't work.
Varnish or Shellac	Paint without pigment. Usually oil-based. Glossy finish.	Wood	Provides a protective finish without adding color.	Slow drying.
Lacquer	Glossy varnish.	Wood	Provides a protective and durable finish.	Hard to remove later.
Polyurethane	Water-based clear coating.	Wood	Provides a protective and durable finish. Dries quickly.	None.

PAINT CHART: FINISHES

FINISH	WHAT IT IS	WHERE & WHEN TO USE
Flat	A flat finish gives no shine or luster to a wall.	Bedrooms, family room. Any room where you want a warm, flat feeling. Don't use it in a room that requires a lot of cleaning, as it is difficult to clean up if it gets dirty. Looks good in any color. It's a great way to cover up imperfections in the wall, as there is no reflection to emphasize it.
Eggshell	Actually, it is just like it sounds— like the surface of an egg. It is mainly flat, but has a tiny bit of luster.	Same as flat.
Satin	A step up in luster from the eggshell finish. This finish will give you a little shine, without any glare.	This finish is easier to clean, but you have to be careful not to scrub too much, as you will take off the finish. Use in most rooms of the home (bedrooms, office, hallway, family room). Where you use it depends a lot on personal preference.
Semi-gloss	A step up in shine from the satin finish. This finish gives a little more shine and tiny bit of glare.	Same as satin.
Gloss (or High-gloss)	A glossy finish provides shine, luster, and reflection, making the room appear brighter.	Use in bathrooms and kitchens. This does not absorb kitchen greases or bathroom condensation as much as other finishes. Also use in playrooms. This is the easiest finish to keep clean, as you can just wipe off anything. Not good for rooms that you want to appear warm.

While investigating paints to share with you, I discovered something that especially fascinated me—"anti-climb paint." It is so cool that this actually exists! Manufacturers make a paint that, while it appears normal when you apply it, dries to a slippery finish so that burglars cannot climb whatever it's painted on (drainpipes, ledges, etc.).

Always read the label on paints. The label will give you a lot of useful information and keep up with the changing elements of paint. It will usually give you drying time, surface preparation information, average area of coverage, and warning information. The label is your friend!

Common Terms

Let's take this opportunity to go over a couple of painting terms. *Cutting in* means "edging" paint, or starting the corners and the outer edges of a wall with a paint brush to bring the paint in a few inches so that it is easy to do the rest with a roller. *Blue painter's tape* is the blue masking tape that you will find in the painting section of hardware stores. It comes in a variety of widths. It allows you to mask off areas that you do not wish to paint (such as baseboards, moldings, windowsills, etc.). It is easy to remove and will not pull off the underlying paint, which is what mainly differentiates it from regular masking tape. I've used regular masking tape when I've been in a bind and have always been sorry for doing so. It pulls off the paint on the taped surface, just making more work.

How Much Paint Should I Buy?

Generally, one gallon of paint will cover approximately four hundred square feet of wall space. Keep in mind, however, that this is just a rough estimate. Some paint (usually higher quality paint) will cover more area, and some paint may take two or three coats to cover that same amount of space. When buying paint, talk to the customer-service representative. He or she will be able to tell you how well the paint will perform, and you can thus buy accordingly.

How do you tell what four hundred square feet of wall

space looks like? Well, you measure your wall. Multiply (yes, you *do* need it after school) the length of the wall by the height to get the square footage. For instance, if your wall is ten feet long and eight feet high, your square footage is eighty feet.

There is interior paint and exterior paint. Check the label to be sure that you are buying the right paint for the job.

What about trim paint? The trim is usually a different color from the walls of the home. It can be lighter or darker, depending on your preference. For every six gallons of wall paint, you will need one gallon of trim paint. If you have a lot of trim around windows and doors, it might push your need to two gallons per every six. Trim paint is no different from regular paint—except, of course, for the color.

Mixing, Opening, and Preserving Paint

Mix paint thoroughly by shaking it in the can before you open it. If you are going to start immediately after you buy the paint, have the clerk shake the paint in the store's machine. If you have had the paint for some time, turn it over and let it sit for about twenty-four hours before you open it. Paint tends to settle and this will allow the sediment to move around and give the paint a more uniform color. To open the paint can, it is best to use a small opening tool, which you can get from any hardware or paint store. If you are in a pinch, you can use a flat-head screwdriver. Place the tool under the lip of the lid, and lift a tiny bit of lid equally all the way around. Once you do open it, mix the paint with a stir stick, or any clean piece of wood.

If you need to put the paint away until the next day to finish the project, simply place the lid evenly back on the paint can. Holding your hand in the middle of the lid, apply pressure while lightly tapping the rim all the way around with a rubber mallet. If you have lost the lid or want to cover a bucket, put it in a plastic bag and seal it off so that no air can creep in. If it is water-based paint, you can pour a shallow layer of water over the top and just mix it in the next day.

How Do I Choose a Paintbrush?

Choosing a paintbrush all depends on what you are using it for. Always buy quality brushes. When you skimp, the brush tends to fall apart, and you will end up having to pull loose bristles out of your paint job, leaving you with a less-than-perfect look. For water-based paints, you can choose all-purpose brushes. For oil-based paint, choose brushes made with animal hair, such as ox or hog. Most brushes will be marked for their best application. Look at the packages before you buy.

It's best to keep a range of clean brushes on hand, including 2½-, 3-, and 4-inch flat brushes as well as tapered sash brushes. Here is a detailed list of paintbrushes and their uses:

Walls For walls (cutting around the sections you will roll), choose a 3-inch to 5-inch paintbrush with straight edges. These can be called wall brushes or professional paintbrushes, and are designed to carry lots of paint and distribute it widely.

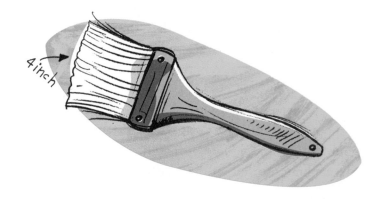

4 inch

Wood For most woodworking projects, choose a two-inch paintbrush with straight edges. These are typically called trim brushes.

Corners and windows When you need to get into tight places, such as corners and windowsills, it is best to choose an angled or tapered paintbrush. Also called sash brushes, these are from 1½ to 2½ inches wide.

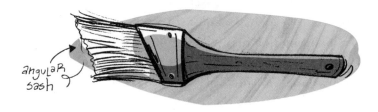

How Do I Choose a Roller?

Invest money in a good, high-quality paint roller base. You can use it for years to come, and even the best ones are fairly inexpensive.

The standard roller is nine inches wide and has a sturdy metal frame. Pick up the roller for a test drive in the hardware store, and buy the one that fits your hand most comfortably. Make sure that the bottom of the roller handle is threaded so that you can attach an extension pole for hard-to-reach places.

Roller covers are disposable and come in various different thicknesses, or "naps." For most interior jobs, you need only a ¼- or ⅜-inch nap. If you have a rough surface (such as stucco or brick), it is best to use a thicker nap (¾-inch or more). Choose a quality roller frame that won't let the cover slip off. Just like a paintbrush, make sure you buy a cover made of quality nap. If you don't, you will end up having to pull tiny fibers out of your paint job.

Before using a roller cover, be sure to rinse it off (with water if using water-based paint or with paint remover if using oil-based) to remove any loose particles or lint. Can you reuse paint rollers? Depending on the quality and the surface, you may be able to use the rollers a few times. But just take a look: you will be able to tell when you can no longer use the roller because it won't roll as well and will begin leaving nap behind on the wall.

For water-based paint, an all-purpose roller cover will work just fine. For oil-based paints, however, you will want to use a more expensive roller cover, such as lamb's wool. If you are painting to a high-gloss finish, try to find a mohair roller cover. It is more expensive but will leave you with a smooth, professional finish.

Painting Interiors

PREPARING INTERIORS

The key to a successful, good-looking paint job is preparation. As with anything in life, when you are more prepared, you tend to be more efficient and to look better! Painting is no exception. Preparation usually takes longer than the actual painting and is thus tempting to skip, but *trust me*. The time you take to properly prepare at the beginning of the job will save you lots of headaches and money in the long run.

If your interior walls have been well maintained, and you are simply going to freshen them up or change the color, then prep time can be kept to a minimum, and may even be as simple as washing the walls.

If the walls are in bad shape, however, be prepared for some serious effort. I once spent two weeks preparing a single bathroom in an old rental apartment; not only were there layers and layers of cheap paint from years of quick-fix-property-manager jobs, but the paint was covering wallpaper from the 1950s. By the time I got to the paper, I felt like I was on an archaeological dig! Apart from the walls, the studio apartment had old ornate plaster ceilings—beautiful, but a nightmare to scrape back all the flaky, hanging paint.

TUFF METER: 2

 TIMER: Preparation time depends not only on how much square footage of wall you are dealing with, but also on the condition of the room. It could be anywhere from a couple of hours to a couple of weeks—or more.

TUFF TOOLS: Drop cloths, small putty knife, sandpaper (100 grit or similar)

 SHOPPING LIST: Painter's masking tape ($5.59), joint compound or wall putty ($4.95), sandpaper ($1.89/6 sheets)

 TOTAL PRICE: $12.43 $20–$30/hour

How to prepare interiors:

1. Remove all furniture and rugs, or move these items to the middle of the room and cover them with a sheet.

2. Remove all pictures, shelves, hooks, curtain rods, brackets, and any other moveable items from the walls. Be sure to keep all screws, nails, etc., with the item so they do not get lost.

Tape screws to the objects you remove so that the hardware stays with the objects.

3. Remove cover plates from electrical outlets and switches. Be sure to keep all screws with their plates.

4. Protect any other item in room with either a drop cloth or tape. You can use the blue painter's tape for baseboards, corners, windowsills, or any area that you would like to mask off.

5. Fix the walls by repairing any small holes. Fill these with joint compound or putty with a small putty knife. Once it's dry, sand it until smooth with 100-grit sandpaper. Seal these spots with primer.

6. Wash down all walls with a sponge or wet rag.

REMOVING INDOOR PAINT

In this book, I explain how to remove paint from outdoor wood surfaces but do not explain how to remove paint from indoor surfaces. Don't fear, this is not an oversight; there's a good reason for the omission. You typically do not remove paint on indoor surfaces. You simply paint over walls. If you have a *wood* surface indoors, you can follow the same instructions for removing paint from wood that I lay out in the "Outdoor" section. For normal walls, just get out your paint and get to work! If you have a dark wall, you may want to use primer to cover it before you add the color of your dreams.

PRIMING INDOOR SURFACES

You should prime most surfaces that you intend to paint. If you are covering an old paint job, and the color is not too dark, you can get away with not priming. Priming is just as it sounds—it "primes" or prepares the wall for paint. You should *definitely* prime any wall surface that you have just repaired and unfinished wood that you intend to paint.

How do you prime? Priming is just painting, so follow the directions below. Instead of paint, use primer!

PAINTING INDOOR SURFACES

TUFF METER: 1

TIMER: Depends on how much you have to paint, but a normal 10 x 10 foot room should take about 6 hours, with 2 hours of preparation time.

TUFF TOOLS: Roller frame, roller tray, 2-inch paintbrush, extension handle

SHOPPING LIST: Roller sleeve covers (short or medium wool; $8.49/six), disposable tray liners ($5.48/five), interior paint ($12.99), 2-inch paintbrush ($2.99)

TOTAL PRICE: $26.96

$20–$30/hour, plus materials

TUFF CHIX DICTIONARY

A primer is a sealant used to prepare a surface for painting or similar process. There are primers made for all types of surfaces. They serve several purposes. If you use the correct primer for the job, the paint will last longer, and it will take fewer coats of paint to cover the surface. It also helps paint stick to the surface. Primer comes in both water-based and oil-based formulas. It is best to use the formula that coincides with your paint choice. You can even tint the primer, and that way it will usually only take one coat of your paint to cover the surface.

Why is primer so important? Primer seals the wall and makes a clean and even backdrop for a successful paint job. It may seem like an unnecessary step, but trust me—it's very important and will save you time and money every time you paint.

PAINTING WITH A PAINTBRUSH

Let the painting begin! Now that your room is prepared, you are ready to start painting. The best way to paint is from top to bottom, mainly because if paint should drip down the wall, you can easily smooth the surface and retouch. Start at the top near the ceiling with a two-inch paintbrush. This is where you do the "cutting in" described earlier. Use this brush to paint the corners and edges, including near the baseboard, doors, and window trim. You can then fill in the rest of the surface with a paint roller.

How to paint with a paintbrush:

1. Dip the paintbrush into the paint.

2. Pull the paintbrush along the side of the container to remove any excess paint and avoid drips.

3. Use long, even strokes to spread the paint on the painting surface. Make sure that you do not have any drips or buildup.

4. Keep using the brush until the strokes become dry.

5. Redip the brush into the paint and continue.

Tuff Tip

Take a large nail with a very sharp point and make five or six tiny holes all along the rim of the paint can. This allows the paint to drain back into the can when you brush off excess, instead of it spilling over the sides.

$Tuff\ Tip$

There are a couple of different ways to apply paint to your roller. The first is by using a paint tray as explained above. Another is to hang a paint grate or bucket screen over a five-gallon bucket of paint. You can dip the roller into the paint, run it along the grate, and get a nice, even distribution of paint over the roller. If you do this, add to your Tuff Tools list a large bucket and bucket screen.

PAINTING WITH A ROLLER

For a large surface, rolling is the best way to achieve fast and efficient results with ample coverage. When purchasing a roller sleeve (or cover), don't skimp. Spend the money and get a higher quality sleeve. It will pay off in the long run. Use rolling to fill in the central part of the surface after you have done the cutting in on the corners and edges with a paint-brush.

How to paint with a roller:

1. Remove any excess lint from the roller sleeve

2. If you are using water-based latex paint, run the sleeve under water. This opens up the fibers and allows paint to penetrate. Use mineral spirits if you are using oil-based paints.

3. Squeeze any excess liquid from the roller

4. Fill the paint tray—not too deep—with paint.

5. To properly put paint on the roller, dip it into the paint then use the textured ramp of the paint tray to roll the roller back and forth and evenly distribute the paint. Your roller should be covered with just enough paint, but not so much that it is dripping or running.

6. On the surface, make an upward roll. Continue rolling both up and down in about 4-foot sections, at a slight

6

diagonal. Be careful not to go so fast that you splatter paint.

7. Use the roller until the strokes become dry.

8. Then redip the roller in the paint and continue.

Tuff Tip

Use a large plastic bag to cover an entire paint tray. Pour the paint into the tray, over the plastic bag. That way, when you are complete, you just turn the bag inside out and throw the mess away.

Painting Wood

Have you ever noticed when you get a manicure that they always buff your nails before applying the nail polish? The same is true when you paint wood. You want to rough up the surface area so that the paint has a better opportunity to stick. Do this with a fine-grit sandpaper. (See chart on p. 75.)

PREPARING WOOD

TUFF METER: 2

 TIMER: The time will depend on the size of the area you need to prepare.

TUFF TOOLS: Scraper or small putty knife, heat gun

 SHOPPING LIST: Wood filler (color to match wood; $3.79), sandpaper (150 grit; $1.89/6 sheets)

TOTAL PRICE: $5.68   **$20/hour**

SANDPAPER CHART

GRITS	MEANING	USED FOR
35–60	Coarse	Very heavy sanding, stripping, and roughing up the surface
80–120	Medium	Medium smoothing of the surface. Roughs up the surface so that paint can adhere. Removes smaller imperfections in surface.
150–180	Fine	Very light sanding and smoothing. Used for final sanding before buffing and/or finishing.
220–240	Very fine	Extremely light sanding and smoothing. Used for sanding between coats of stain or sealer. Gives a light buffing.
280–320	Extra fine	Even lighter sanding and smoothing. Used to remove tiny imperfections or dust spots before the finished coats of stain or sealer.
360–600	Super fine	*Fine* sanding and smoothing. More like buffing for a shiny finish (like you would use on your nails). This can be used to remove miniscule surface imperfections and tiny scratches.

How to prepare a wood surface for painting:

1. Apply wood filler to any area needing repair. Let it dry according to the manufacturer's label. You can also test an area by running your finger across it. If nothing sticks to your finger, it's dry.

2. Once the wood filler has dried, sand the area with fine sandpaper (150 grit) until smooth or until it matches the surface of the wood.

3. Wipe the area clean with a damp cloth.

4. Apply paint.

If you have wood that you would like to repaint, you may want to simply paint over the existing paint, which is good for a variety of projects. This simply requires cleaning the wood with soap and water before getting started, but don't forget to lightly sand.

For more detailed projects, it is best to strip the wood and start fresh to avoid a thick, unattractive buildup. There are two main ways of doing this: heat stripping and chemical stripping.

HEAT STRIPPING

TUFF METER: 3

 TIMER: The time will depend on how large your project is.

TUFF TOOLS: Scraper or small putty knife, heat gun

 SHOPPING LIST: Sandpaper (both rough and fine grits; $1.89–$2.49/6 sheets)

TOTAL PRICE: $1.89   **$15/hour**

How to heat strip wood:

1. Hold the heat gun about 4 inches away from the wood, using slight back-and-forth motions.

2. The paint should start to soften and begin to blister. Be careful not to overheat the paint since it will turn into a paste that is hard to remove. Remember, too, that wood is a flammable material and can be scorched or catch fire.

3. Remove the heat and start scraping the paint from wood with a metal scraper.

4. Repeat steps until the paint is mostly removed.

5. Use the rough sandpaper to sand down any sections that still have paint.

6. Use the fine sandpaper over the entire surface to create a clean, smooth surface for painting.

7. Wipe down the wood with a damp cloth.

CHEMICAL STRIPPING

Follow the directions on the chemical stripping agent, since they vary slightly, but for a general guideline, follow the steps below.

How to chemically strip wood:

1. Using a paintbrush, apply the recommended amount of stripping agent to the wood's surface. You can usually be pretty generous with your application. Use a disposable, inexpensive paintbrush for this job.

2. Let the agent sit for a while until the paint starts to blister.

TUFF METER: 3

TIMER: The time will depend on the size of the project and the detail of the wood.

TUFF TOOLS: Scraper or small putty knife (or steel wool), paintbrush

SHOPPING LIST: Chemical stripping agent ($47.98/gallon, 2-pack), sandpaper (both rough and fine grits; $1.89–$2.49)

TOTAL PRICE: $52.36

$20/hour, plus materials

3. Then use a scraper or putty knife to scrape away the paint. You can also use steel wool to scrub away the paint.

4. Use a cloth to remove the scraped paint as you go because you don't want to scrape the paint back into the wood.

5. Use some stripping agent on a cloth or steel wool to remove any residual paint and to clean the surface.

6. Wipe down the wood surface with a damp cloth or sponge.

> **SAFETY:** Wear chemical-resistant rubber gloves, splashproof goggles, rubber footwear, and a dual-cartridge respirator.

PATCHING VARNISHED WOOD

How to patch varnished wood:

1. Apply wood filler to any area needing repair. Let it dry according to the manufacturer's label. You can also test an area by running your finger across it. If nothing sticks to your finger, it's dry.

TUFF METER: **2**

TIMER: The time it takes will depend on the size of the area to be patched.

TUFF TOOLS: Scraper or small putty knife, paintbrush

SHOPPING LIST: Wood filler (color to match wood; $3.79), sandpaper (150 grit; $1.89/6 sheets)

TOTAL PRICE: $5.68

$15–$20/hour, plus materials

2. Once the wood filler has dried, sand the area with fine sandpaper (150 grit) until smooth or until it matches the surface of the wood.

3. With a damp cloth, wipe the area clean.

4. Add varnish with either a rag or a paintbrush.

Painting Concrete Floors

Preparation is especially important when the surface to be painted is a concrete floor, such as in a laundry room or workshop. First you will want to repair any cracks or holes (see "Cement and Concrete," p. 33). You will next need to prepare the concrete with a muriatic acid solution. This process is called "etching." It's similar to etching glass—scraping off a bit of the top so that the paint has something to adhere to. Caution: muriatic acid is strong enough to burn skin and eyes. Before you begin the etching process, put on the proper safety gear. If you can't ventilate the work area, wear a dual-cartridge respirator.

TUFF METER: 6

TIMER: 2 hours, with wait time in between steps

TUFF TOOLS: Broom, scraper, stiff-bristled brush, vacuum

SHOPPING LIST: Cleaning solution ($22.99), muriatic acid ($7.12/gallon), sponge ($2.99)

TOTAL PRICE: $33.10

$25–$30/hour,
plus materials

How to prepare and paint a concrete floor:

1. First, sweep and scrape off the dirt from the floor. Clean off any grease, oil, and other contaminants using a cleaning solution.

2. Rinse the floor well to remove all traces of the cleaning solution.

3. Mix the solution to etch the floor by adding 1 part muriatic acid to 3 parts water. Do it in this order—do NOT add the water to the acid.

4. Apply the solution, using 1 gallon per 100 square feet, and scrub the floor with a stiff-bristled brush. Leave the solution on the floor until it stops bubbling.

5. Rinse the floor thoroughly with clean water. Wipe it down with a damp sponge mop to eliminate puddles.

6. If the floor isn't dry in four hours, repeat the rinsing procedure.

7. After the floor is completely dry, vacuum it to remove any powder residue left by the muriatic acid solution.

8. You can now paint the floor with an alkyd or urethane-latex floor and deck enamel. It is best to paint with a roller and long pole. First paint the edges then work from the wall farthest from the door back toward the door.

3

FLOORS

Repairing Hardwood Floors

Most DIY books bury the fabulous subject of natural wood flooring in the pages at the back of the book, starting instead with how to fix cracked or chipped tile or a tear in vinyl flooring. (We'll get to the more tedious stuff too—don't worry!)

I'm starting this section with how to repair and completely revitalize hardwood flooring because it's not only *much* easier than you think, it's also one of the best ways to change the entire look of a room and to improve the value of your home.

One warning, though, before you start: sanding will get dust *everywhere*. It's such a fine mist of dust, it will be in your toothbrush in the back bathroom before you know it. So hang plastic over as many places as you can to contain the mess.

With a true natural wood floor, you can refinish it every couple of years, if you're up to it, because a true wood floor is pretty thick, leaving you many layers to play with. But be careful that your "wood" floor is not actually veneer, which is usually only an eighth of an inch of wood, with plywood underneath. You can *maybe* sand veneer down once, but I wouldn't recommend it. Veneer, or laminate, wood floors are usually really shiny. They look like fake wood. With real wood, you'll see the grain, and you'll see individual pieces. With veneer, you will see grain that looks like it's painted on, and usually pieces of the flooring will be attached to one another. Older homes tend to have real wood; newer homes, built in the eighties on, often have laminate.

DETERMINE YOUR FINISH

To help you maintain or refinish your hardwood floor, you should know how the floor has been finished. The finish is the hard, shiny coat that protects the floor and is applied on top of any stain. If you don't know what kind of finish you have, test it using a couple of soft cloths, one dampened with denatured alcohol (menthylated spirits, for example) and the other with lacquer, or paint thinner. This is an important step, especially with repair. Don't worry, once you have repaired the floor, you can apply the same finish to complete the flawless look.

How to determine your finish:

1. In a clean, inconspicuous area of the floor, rub the alcohol in a small circle. If the floor's finish starts to come off, it's probably shellac.

2. If the alcohol doesn't work, but the thinner does, the finish is lacquer.

3. If neither solvent works, the finish is a varnish, probably polyurethane.

CHOOSING STAINS AND FINISHES

I really love dark stains—I have mahogany on my own floors—but you can pick what's in fashion or follow your personal preference or how the color matches the rest of your house.

The same goes for varnishes; it depends what you're going for. For example, if you have an old cabin, you're not going to want a high-gloss finish. You're going to want a matt finish or semigloss.

I always check with my local hardware store and ask someone who knows their stuff about stains and varnishes because new ones are coming out all the time. A knowledge-able salesperson will also be able to advise you on the best finishes for various climates.

Not that advice is always foolproof. The first time I did my hardwood floors, I asked the guy in the store what kind of finish I should buy—choosing between semigloss and high gloss. He told me that high gloss would look like I was walking into a high school basketball court—too shiny. So I got semigloss—and it barely shined! After putting in so much work on a floor, I *wanted* it to shine. It's personal preference, of course, but I went back three months later and got the high gloss, and it did *not* look like a basketball court—probably because I had old wood floors. They were shiny, but it just looked like they were clean.

Again, take advice, but at the end of the day, always trust what you like. And sometimes, you just have to experiment.

When shopping for stains and varnishes, I usually use the big hardware stores because of the selection they have; sometimes the smaller stores will only have two different types of varnish. The bigger stores will have ten or twelve different kinds, with a wider price range to fit your budget.

If you're really on a tight budget, you may want to get the cheapest varnish, instead of the best, most expensive varnish. This might apply if you're doing a "flipper," and getting rid of the property; you may just want the quickest fix, the

Tuff Tips

- The easiest way to apply stain is to put it on rags and rub it on the floor. You can also mop it on.
- Varnish is generally easier to mop on. Some companies have their own mops specific to particular products.
- It's common sense, but start in the farthest corner and work your way out of the room. You have to let it dry, typically for forty-eight hours before you put furniture back, though usually you can walk on it after twenty-four hours.
- Put felt pads on the bottom of your furniture. That way, when you want to move it or adjust it later, you won't ruin or scratch your beautiful hardwood floors.

one that is going to cost you the least amount of money. If this is for your own house, and you don't want to revarnish or change the look often, then get the very best quality stains and varnishes because you'll save money in the long run. If it's an investment property or a rental, then you'll probably be looking at the cheaper options.

REPAIRING ANY HOLES

Holes in hardwood floors can be filled with wood putty, but trying to apply wood putty directly over sealant or varnish is a bad idea. Just as buffing your nails helps nail polish stick, you need to rough up your wood floor so that the putty sticks. Always start with a rough-grit sandpaper (the thicker the varnish, the rougher the grit) and move up to finer grits. Also make sure to match the color of your putty to the color of your floor (oak, cherry, etc).

TUFF METER: 2

 TIMER: The time will depend on the size of the area with holes. About 30 minutes per hole.

TUFF TOOLS: Scraper

 SHOPPING LIST: Wood filler (color to match wood; $3.79), sandpaper (65 and 150 grit; $1.89/6 sheets)

 TOTAL PRICE: $5.68 $20/hour

How to repair a hole:

1. Take a little sandpaper in your hand and rough up the area around the hole. Start with a rougher grit sandpaper (e.g., 65 grit) to remove any varnish, and go to a finer grit as you need a smoother finish (to 150 grit, for example). Always sand *with* the grain.

2. With a putty knife or scraper tool, add wood putty to the sanded repair area, scrape flat and let dry according to the manufacturer's recommendations.

3. Once dry, sand the putty in the direction of the grain of the wood. If the dried putty has significantly contracted or shrunk, you may need to repeat the process with another coat of wood filler.

go with the grain   **3**

4. Apply the finish, trying to match the varnish or polyurethane, or whatever it had on it, to the rest of wood.

SANDING A HARDWOOD FLOOR

Sanding will make your old hardwood floor look new. You can also alter the entire look and feel of a room just by changing the varnish color.

Typically, for most finishes, you can use an electric square sander. This is a large, almost lawn-mower-like machine that you push and is very easy to use. As a general rule, use the finest (least gritty) sandpaper that's effective for the job. Start with thicker grit sandpaper and move up to the finer grits.

against the grain leaves scratches!

For wood floors that have a particularly thick or stubborn coating (such as leftover felt or carpet glue), you will need a powerful drum sander. Some people suggest using mineral spirits to remove heavy buildups of varnish or tar or glue on the floor. I've tried it, and it just made a paste all over the floor! It's very messy and takes more time than sanding, so I

TUFF METER: 7

TIMER: It depends on the size of your room, but this will take you a couple of days.

TUFF TOOLS: Drum sander or square sander, hand sander (or edge sander), scraper, vacuum

SHOPPING LIST: Sanding belts ($9.49–$22.99/five) or discs ($40/10-pack), cloth, floor finish ($6.99–$69.99), plastic sheets ($6.99), painter's tape ($5.59)

TOTAL PRICE: $29.06
plus sander rental

$2–$3/sq. ft.,
plus material and rental

wouldn't recommend it. The drum sander is harder to use than the square sander, and takes a lot of care, but you can do it.

How to sand wood floors using a drum sander:

1. Vacuum the floor thoroughly before each stage of sanding.

2. Start with 80-grit sandpaper, and position the drum sander about a foot from the wall. With the drum raised above the floor, start the machine and move it forward, slowly lowering the drum. Sand in the direction of the floorboards, to within 1 foot of the end wall,

Tuff Tips

- Because sanding removes the wood's aged surface, or patina, it's often difficult to blend a repaired area with the rest of the floor. If you're planning a major repair, particularly if it's in a conspicuous area of the room, consider refinishing the entire floor.
- Always sand *with* the grain of the wood. Doing so will assure a good surface. Going against the grain will leave you with scrapes and scratches.

and raise the drum with the sander in motion. The start, middle, and finish should be one fluid motion. You *must* sand in the direction of the boards! Make a pass as long as you can, traveling in the same direction.

3. Return to your starting point and begin the second pass, overlapping the first by one-half its width.

4. Use a hand sander to get to the edges and corners of hardwood floors. (Hand sanders fit in the palm of your hand.)

2

5. The first stage of sanding should remove most of the old finish. Switch to a 120-grit sandpaper and resand the entire floor.

6. Repeat the sanding process, using finer sandpaper (150–180 grit) to remove scratches left by the coarser papers.

4

7. Sand along the edges with the hand sander, using the same sequence of sandpapers used with the drum sander.

8. Scrape the old finish from hard-to-reach areas. Hand sand those areas smooth.

Tuff Tips

- You can rent a square sander from a tool-rental joint. Ask for a demonstration of how to use it: it's easy, but having someone show you first makes it even easier. The drum sander is a bit harder. Stay away from large orbital (circular) sanders. These are very hard to control and can whip you around.
- Do the whole floor before switching over to a finer grit sandpaper. Make sure to cover all areas. A lot of times you'll see uneven floors, and it's often because of leftover varnish where a floor hasn't been sanded evenly.

9. Vacuum the floor thoroughly. Then wipe the floor with a damp cloth to remove dust just before you are ready to stain/varnish. You can stain it, or if you like the natural wood, you can just put a varnish over it.

10. Apply the topcoat of your choice. Polyurethane is a good product for a clear, durable finish.

How to sand wood floors using a square sander:

1. The method is pretty much the same as the drum sander, only *much easier*. Use the square sander in 4 x 4 foot sections. You do *not* have to move in the direction of the grain, since the sander itself moves back and forth.

2. Move the sander over these 4 x 4 sections until the entire floor surface is done, changing up to finer grit sandpaper with every pass.

REMOVING STAINS

TUFF METER: 5

TIMER: 3 hours

TUFF TOOLS: Sandpaper (100 grit and 220 grit)

SHOPPING LIST: Oxalic acid crystals ($3.25), borax ($9.95), wood stain (to match your floor; $19/gallon)

TOTAL PRICE: $32.20

$30–$50/hour, plus materials and stain

Water and other liquids can penetrate deep into the grain of hardwood floors, leaving dark stains that are sometimes impossible to remove by sanding. Instead, try bleaching the wood with oxalic acid, which is available in crystal form at home centers or paint stores.

How to remove stains from hardwood floors:

SAFETY: Wear rubber gloves.

1. Remove the floor's finish by sanding the stained area.

2. In a disposable cup, dissolve the recommended amount of oxalic acid crystals in water.

3. Wearing rubber gloves, pour the mixture over the stained area, taking care to cover only the darkened wood.

4. Let the liquid stand for 1 hour. Repeat the application, if necessary.

5. Wash the area with a solution of 2 tablespoons borax in 1 pint of water to neutralize the acid.

6. Rinse with water, and let the wood dry.

7. Sand the area smooth.

8. Apply several coats of wood stain until the bleached area matches the finish of the surrounding floor.

ELIMINATING SQUEAKS

Wood expands and shrinks according to weather conditions—especially humidity—causing floorboards to rub against each

Tuff Tip

One trick, for a temporary fix, is to put some baby powder between the boards that squeak. Step on the boards in a bouncing action to allow the powder to seep into the joints.

other and against the nails holding them in place, and thus to squeak. It pays to check, however, whether the source of persistent squeaky boards is more than a change in weather. Sometimes shifting or squeaking boards can indicate a bigger problem, like leaking pipes or drains. Be sure to check under the floor to make sure it is free from water damage or rot.

Although there are little tricks to get rid of those squeaks, sanding and refinishing the floor is not one of them, so don't let any professional talk you into something you don't need and that won't fix the problem. Little tricks are good, but to truly fix the problem, you will need to uproot your flooring and repair what's going on underneath it.

Repairing Carpet

I remember being so afraid of this topic. I thought if the carpet was damaged, there was just nothing I could do. I found that once you have rented the proper tools, it's really easy to do. Plus, your helpful salesperson at the carpet-tool-rental place will give you lots of tips and even show you what to do.

TUFF METER: 3

 TIMER: 1 hour

TUFF TOOLS: Small scissors, utility knife, ruler

 SHOPPING LIST: Seam adhesive ($6.49/50-foot roll), double-faced carpet tape ($15/25 feet)

 TOTAL PRICE: $21.49 $30/hour, plus materials

SNAGS

Do *not* pull! If you pull a thread of carpet, you will most likely pull more than you want and ruin that section. Instead, trim the snag with small scissors.

SMALL BURNS OR STAINS

Burns and stains are the most common carpeting problems. You can clip away the burned fibers of superficial burns, using small scissors. But if you have bigger problems—keep on reading.

SPOT DAMAGE

To patch deeper burns, as well as indelible stains, cut away and replace the damaged area. Only do this, however, if you have some scraps or remnants of the same carpet (perhaps left over from when it was installed).

How to patch carpet:

1. Mark out the section you want to remove. It will be easiest to cut a square out of the carpet just larger than the damaged area.

2. Take a ruler and separate the carpet fibers. This will allow you to cut in a straight line and to cut *only* the base of the carpet.

3. Take your utility knife and cut along the ruler. Move the ruler around until you have cut out a perfect square.

4. Remove the damaged piece and vacuum the open area.

Instead of double-faced carpet tape, you can use your crafty hot glue gun! Although not recommended by carpet installers, it will do the job just fine.

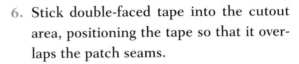

5. Take the piece of damaged carpet that you just cut out and use it to trace its dimensions on the backside of the replacement remnant, or patch.

6. Stick double-faced tape into the cutout area, positioning the tape so that it overlaps the patch seams.

7. Press the patch into place. Make sure the direction of the carpet weave or pattern matches the existing carpet. To seal the seam and prevent unraveling, apply seam adhesive to the edges of the patch.

carpet
tape

Damaged
carpet

RESTRETCHING LOOSE CARPET

Carpeting that isn't glued down is held around the perimeter of a room by wood strips with metal pins that grip the carpet backing. To repair loose carpets, you'll need to rent a "knee kicker," a stretching tool to pull the carpet tight and reattach the edges to the strips. These can be found at rental centers and carpet distributors.

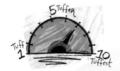

TUFF METER: 7

TIMER: The time will depend on the size of the area.

TUFF TOOLS: Wallboard knife

SHOPPING LIST: Knee kicker (can rent; $10/day)

TOTAL PRICE: $65

$30/hour, plus materials

How to restretch carpet:

1. Turn the knob on the head of the knee kicker to adjust the depth of the prongs. The prongs should extend far enough to grab the carpet backing without penetrating through the padding.

2. Starting from a corner or near a point where the carpet is firmly attached, press the knee kicker head into the carpet, about 2 inches from the wall. Thrust your knee into the cushion of the knee kicker to force the carpet toward the wall.

3. Tuck the carpet edge into the space between the wood strip and the baseboard, using a 4-inch wallboard knife.

REGLUING LOOSE SEAMS

Most carpets are held together at the edges with heat-activated seam tape. The tape comes in rolls and has hardened glue on one face. You will need to rent a "seam iron."

TUFF METER: 4

TIMER: 1 hour

TUFF TOOLS: Scissors, weighted boards (or phone books)

SHOPPING LIST: Seam iron (can rent) ($19.99–$79.99), seam tape ($6.49/50 feet)

TOTAL PRICE: $26.48　　　　　　　　　　$20–$30/hour, plus materials

How to reglue loose seams:

2

1. Remove the old tape from under the carpet seam.

2. Cut a strip of new seam tape, and place it under the carpet so it is centered along the seam with the adhesive facing up.

3. Plug in the seam iron, and let it heat up. Seam irons work like curling irons and regular irons, but they vary in the amount of time needed to heat up. Check the manufacturer's instructions to see how long you should wait for it to heat up.

4. Pull up both edges of the carpet, and set the hot iron squarely onto the tape. Wait about 30 seconds for the glue to melt.

5. Move the iron farther along the seam, as necessary.

6. Quickly press the edges of the carpet together into the melted glue behind the iron. If anything goes wrong you have only 30 seconds to repeat the process.

7. Separate the pile to make sure no fibers are stuck in the glue and that the seam is tight.

8. Place weighted boards or phone books over the seam to keep it flat while the glue sets.

Repairing Vinyl Flooring

Vinyl floors are popular because they're easy to clean and maintain. Today's high-quality vinyl floor coverings don't require any regular care beyond frequent sweeping and mopping. But vinyl does get divots, holes, and tears. The only way to really repair it is to cut out the damaged section and replace it with a patch. It's pretty easy to fix vinyl if you have remnants and you can match it; if you don't, there's not a lot you can do.

With vinyl tile, it's best to replace the damaged tiles. With sheet vinyl, you can fuse the surface or patch in new material.

SMALL CUTS AND SCRATCHES

Small cuts and scratches can be fused permanently and nearly invisibly with liquid seam sealer, a clear compound that's available wherever vinyl flooring is sold.

TUFF METER: 2

TIMER: 20 minutes

TUFF TOOLS: Cloth

SHOPPING LIST: Lacquer thinner ($2.30), liquid seam sealer ($9.86/9 oz. bottle)

TOTAL PRICE: $12.16 $20–$30/hour, plus materials

How to fix small cuts and scratches in vinyl flooring:

1. Clean the area with lacquer thinner and a soft cloth.

2. When it's dry, squeeze a thin bead of liquid seam sealer into the cut or scratch.

3. Use your finger (wearing a rubber glove) and lightly smooth out the edges, if needed.

4. Let dry—and voilà!

> **SAFETY:** Wear rubber gloves

If your flooring is all one color, you can fix gouges another way. Shred a piece of your vinyl flooring in a food grater. Take the shavings and mix them with a small amount of clear nail polish, drop by drop, until you have a pastelike mixture. Wearing a rubber glove, put this mixture into the groove and squish it into place. Let dry.

LARGER TEARS AND BURNS

If you have larger tears or burns, you will need to do a little bit more.

Repairing a section of vinyl flooring is closely related to replacing a ceramic tile, except that you make the "tiles." You will cut out the damaged area and glue in a patch cut from matching flooring. Here's how.

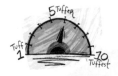

TUFF METER: 6

TIMER: 1 hour

TUFF TOOLS: Carpenter's square (or ruler), utility knife (or pocket knife), leftover remnants of vinyl flooring, notched trowel

SHOPPING LIST: Lacquer thinner ($2.30), liquid seam sealer ($9.86), vinyl floor adhesive ($19.99/gallon), masking tape ($1.44)

TOTAL PRICE: $33.59 $20–$30/hour, plus materials

How to fix larger tears and burns in vinyl flooring:

SAFETY: Wear rubber gloves

1. Clean the section of flooring to be replaced thoroughly with soap and water or lacquer thinner. Then wait until it is completely dry.

2. Take a piece of replacement flooring and cut it slightly larger than the damaged area. If the flooring is checkered or patterned, make sure your replacement piece matches the pattern.

3. Place this piece over the damaged floor and secure it to the floor with masking tape.

4. Take a utility knife and carefully cut through *both* sections of flooring. This will ensure that your replacement piece will be the *exact* same size. Use your ruler to make straight lines if you have a straight pattern. If you have an asymmetrically patterned floor (like flowers), trace around an item in the pattern. Following the pattern (such as cutting around a flower) will hide any seams that might otherwise show.

cut line

4

5. Remove the masking tape and both pieces of flooring. Discard the damaged piece. If the piece is stuck to the floor, use your utility knife to pry the edges free, and scrape underneath with a scraper until you have set it free.

6. Make sure the area underneath the removed piece is clean and free of debris. You may need to scrap off any old glue.

7. Wearing rubber gloves, take vinyl adhesive with your notched trowel and spread it on the area. If the area is too small to use a trowel, use a fork to create similar lines. Look at the manufacturer's instructions on the adhesive and allow it to set up for the appropriate amount of time.

vinyl adhesive

7

8. When the adhesive is ready, carefully set the replacement piece of vinyl in place. Press on it lightly and gently. With a damp cloth, wipe away any excess adhesive that creeps up.

9. If you press too hard on vinyl it will pick up irregular pressure and make a dent. The best way to set the patch level and into place is to cover it with a cloth and put a flat-surfaced weight on top of it, such as a large book. Keep this weight in place for as long as the manufacturer's instructions indicate the adhesive needs to completely cure.

10. When the vinyl is cured (it may take a couple of days), remove the weight and the cloth. Clean away any excess adhesive with a damp cloth. You may need to remove pesky adhesive with lacquer thinner.

11. Use your finger (wearing a rubber glove) and lightly smooth out the edges, if needed.

Too big to repair? When vinyl flooring is badly worn or the damage is widespread, the only answer is complete replacement. Although it's possible to add layers of flooring in some situations, it probably won't look that great.

Tile Flooring

Ceramic tile is one of the strongest flooring materials on the market. Why is it so strong? Not only is ceramic tile strong in itself, but the way a tile floor is assembled adds to its strength. First, an underlayment is put into place. This is usually a concrete board or plywood. Then, the tile is set into a cement-based mortar on that underlayment. It has a kind of toothpaste consistency that hardens to hold the tile into

- Keep dirt from getting trapped in grout lines by sealing them about once a year.
- Small cracks in the grout can easily be fixed. Major cracks in grout joints, however, indicate that movement of the floor may be at fault. Whenever you remove tile, check the underlayment. If it's no longer smooth, solid, and level, repair or replace it before replacing the tile.

place. Finally, the spaces between tiles are filled with a thin mortar, or grout, which dries and holds the tiles together. Each of these elements plays a part in maintaining the integrity of the floor.

Although there are significant differences among the various types of ceramic tile, most carry a price tag that reflects ceramic tile's appeal and durability. Ceramic tile is easy to maintain, but that doesn't mean you can ignore it. Many ceramic tiles have a glazed surface that protects the porous clay from staining, but you should protect unglazed ceramic tile from stains and water spots by periodically applying a coat of tile sealer. Repairing the tile when there is a problem will protect your investment for many years, and make you very happy with your flooring (see "Ceramic Tile," p. 46).

4

DOORS

We close them, we open them—doors are a part of our everyday lives. We use them for security, for privacy, and sometimes for decorating. We don't notice them much, until they start giving us trouble.

Many basic door maintenance and repair jobs are straightforward, but they can be awkward because in most cases you need to take the door off its hinges. It is possible to take down a door on your own, but it's much easier if you have someone helping you by holding the door as you remove the hinges. Plus, hinges and pins that have been painted over will give you an extra run for your money!

If you are buying replacement hinges make sure to match materials: hinges come in brass, nickel plate, and silver and in all shapes and sizes. As obvious as it sounds, don't forget to take your old hinges to the hardware store when you go shopping for new ones. You always *think* you will remember what yours look like—until you are there staring at several new, shiny, different ones. Trust me—the memory leaves the brain.

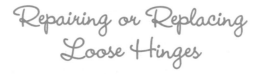

Repairing or Replacing Loose Hinges

Do you have a sticky door? One that won't close all the way? Well, doors will often stick or jam simply because the hinges are loose. Over time, normal use and the weight of the door will pull the screws out of the jamb. Simply putting in longer screws will sometimes fix the problem. Sometimes, however, you may just need to replace the hinges. Not to worry! Replacing the hinges is something you can do.

TUFF METER: 6

TIMER: 30 minutes

TUFF TOOLS: Screwdriver, hammer, utility knife, drill

SHOPPING LIST: Wooden golf tees ($2.99/bag) or dowels (¼-inch; $1.99/12), glue ($3.75), sandpaper ($1.89/6 sheets)

TOTAL PRICE: $10.62 for all materials; you will have leftover for more doors

$50/door,
plus materials

How to repair or replace loose hinges:

1. Remove the door from its hinges by unscrewing the hinges. If you have a helper, have them hold the door in place while you do this. Doors, although not typically heavy, can be cumbersome.

2. Use a flat-head screwdriver and a hammer to first drive the lower hinge pin up and out, and then the upper one.

3. Remove the door and set it aside.

4. Tighten any loose screws. If the wood behind the hinge won't hold the screws, remove the hinges and go to the next step.

5. Coat wooden golf tees or wooden dowels with glue and drive them into the worn screw holes as far as you can. (Or, just choose a new place to drill fresh holes.)

6. Let the glue dry and cut off the excess wood with a utility knife.

2

7. Drill pilot holes into the new wood.

8. Reattach the hinges, using the new wood as a base for the screws.

Tuff Tips

- If the hinge plates are covered with paint, scrape away the paint and expose the screw heads. Remove the screws, then tap the hinge with the hammer to knock it free.
- Instead of going to the trouble of finding golf tees or the right-sized dowels, try pushing a few toothpicks into the old screw hole and snapping them off flush. (You don't need glue for this.) Reinstalling the screws should wedge the toothpicks in so that they're sufficiently tight.
- Replace hinge screws with long (at least three-inch) wood screws. Sometimes these will pull a jamb back into alignment and solve the problem.

PILOT HOLES

You will see the phrase "drill pilot holes" throughout the book. What does it mean?

A pilot hole is a small hole that allows you to drill screws through solid wood easily and keep wood from splitting. I've tried to put a screw through hard wood *without* a pilot hole, and it wasn't pretty. Depending on how long your screw is, it will either bend or break, kill your drill battery, or split the wood. Sure, it's an extra step, but it's a very important extra step that will save you time, money, and frustration in the long run.

You can get pilot hole drill bits at any hardware store. They come in a variety of sizes. I typically use ⅛-inch because most screws (especially drywall screws) will work with that. If you need larger, however, they are available. Take the screw that you intend to use and hold it up to a pilot drill bit. You will want to choose a bit that is slightly smaller than the diameter of the screw.

TUFF METER: 2

TIMER: 5 minutes

TUFF TOOLS: Drill with ⅛-inch drill bit (or drill bit of your chosen size)

SHOPPING LIST: Nothing

TOTAL PRICE: $0   **N/A**

How to drill a pilot hole:

1. Attach your drill bit to the drill.

2. Mark on your project where you would like the hole.

3. Take your drill and drill through the marked area.

4. Remove the drill.

5. Your pilot hole is complete and ready to receive a screw!

Sticky Doors

Over time, wood expands and changes shape in response to different moisture levels in the air. Doors often rub on their trim, causing the familiar sticking door, which is annoying but easy enough to fix.

TUFF METER: 2

TIMER: 30 minutes

TUFF TOOLS: Screwdriver, hammer, belt sander, hand plane and/or palm sander, paintbrush, safety glasses

SHOPPING LIST: Sandpaper ($1.89/6 sheets), varnish ($14.99 and up)

TOTAL PRICE: $16.88 $30/door

How to fix a sticky door:

1. Examine the door and try to determine where it is sticking. First, try tightening any loose hinges—top, bottom, or both—depending on where the door is catching.

2. If the door still sticks, mark the places where it sticks with light pencil or chalk lines.

3. Wearing safety glasses, sand the door gradually at the marked spots, extending the sanding a little beyond the marked boundaries. As frequently as is practical, test the door and only sand until it fits smoothly into the frame.

Tuff Tips

- If the door only sticks in wet weather, wait for a dry period to sand and seal the edges.
- Don't put the new varnish or paint on too thick or you'll be sanding the door all over again!
- If your door rattles, add small rubber cushions to the door stop to narrow the gap between the door and the stop. The cushions can be found in most hardware stores, and will also make a door close more quietly.

4. Wipe the door clean and apply several thin coats of clear wood sealer, varnish, or paint over the sanded spots, to match the original finish. This will prevent moisture from entering and swelling the door again.

How to Add or Replace Weather Stripping

What is weather stripping? It's that rubber stuff that runs all around the sides of your doorjamb and door. A door sweep is the weather stripping at the bottom of an exterior door. Replacing an old or worn door sweep on an exterior door is one of the best and easiest ways to save on energy costs.

How do you know when weather stripping should be replaced? Open your door and inspect all the stripping. Is it in bad shape? Is it peeling, rotted, flaky, cracked, or missing in parts? Are there dents? Press on the rubber or foam. Does it stay depressed? If you answered yes to any of these questions, you need to replace your weather stripping.

Even if the stripping is in good shape, it still may not be laid correctly. If your door allows a draft to pass through it, you need to replace the weather stripping. How can you tell?

Here is a simple way to check for drafts, which I also explained in the "Getting to Know Your House" section in the introduction. Wait until a windy day and hold a tissue up to the doorjamb. If the tissue moves, it's time to replace the weather stripping. This will also keep eight-legged creatures from obtaining easy access.

Weather stripping is made in a variety of different materials and sizes, but the most common is about a ¼-inch wide strip made out of rubber. It can also be applied in a variety of different ways. The easiest method is to buy the self-adhesive type: you just peel away the backing and stick it on. There is also a type of "tack strip," which is attached with nails or staples. There are other application methods and materials (including metal, plastic, foam, and magnetic), but these usually prove to be more difficult, so just stick to the basics on this one. You will be surprised at how easy it is and how much you save on your heating and air-conditioning bill just by applying this simple strip.

 TUFF CHIX DICTIONARY

Weather stripping is that rubber, foam, or other material around your doorjamb and at the bottom of your exterior door. It closes the gap between the door and the jamb, thus sealing the airflow between the inside and outside. It prevents warm air from escaping in winter and cool air from leaking out in summer.

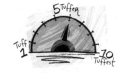

TUFF METER: 6

 TIMER: 45 minutes

TUFF TOOLS: Scraper, chisel, or utility knife

 SHOPPING LIST: Weather stripping ($16.95 for 36" x 84")

TOTAL PRICE: $16.95　　　　　　　　　　　　　　　$50/door, plus materials

How to add or replace weather stripping:

Out with the old:

1. If you currently have bad weather stripping, it will need to be removed before you can get started. Take a scraper, chisel, or utility knife and scrape off the old stripping.

2. If it was held in place with small nails, don't try to remove them. Simply cut the nails flush with the surface, assuring that none stick out past the jamb. If they are still visible, drive them into the jamb by using a bigger nail and tapping slightly with a hammer.

3. Remove all remnants and/or leftover adhesive with the scraper.

4. Clean the area thoroughly with soap and water.

5. Let it dry completely.

In with the new:

1. Measure each side of the doorjamb that needs to be fitted with stripping. Add a couple of inches to your measurements so there is room for play.

2. Cut the new weather stripping to size.

3. Attach the cut pieces to the doorjamb using the method of application that corresponds to the type of

Tuff Tips

• For extra protection from the elements (including those eight-legged ones), install a rubber sweep underneath the door. This is usually a simple exercise of drilling holes and attaching the sweep with screws. There are a couple of different styles of door sweeps to choose from. Some will be easy to install, others may require you to remove the door to install them correctly.

• Rubber weather stripping is not only the easiest to use, but will hold up for a long time and resist the elements. Stay away from felt or foam since they tend to deteriorate quickly.

weather stripping you purchased. Be careful to keep the stripping level and within the jamb.

4. Cut off any excess stripping.

Door Won't Stay Open?

It gets to be very annoying when a door automatically creeps open or closed. There is an easy way to combat this. Take the pin out of the door hinge and bend it slightly. Tap it back into the hinge. This should tighten it enough to keep the door in place.

Installing a Peephole

Ladies, here is an inexpensive and effective way to be more secure in your own home. Peepholes are one of the best and simplest ways to improve security—not to mention the benefits of quietly fending off unwanted salespeople and nosy neighbors!

> **SAFETY:** Wear eye protection whenever you are drilling into wood.

 **TUFF CHIX DICTIONARY**
A peephole is the little "spy" glass in the center of an exterior door that allows you to look outside the door without having to open it.

How to install a peephole:

1. Measure the distance from the floor to eye level. A range of between 58 and 62 inches is comfortable for most adults, but it's a good idea to think about making it accessible to any children in the house—even if this makes it on the low side for you.

TIMER: 30–45 minutes

TUFF TOOLS: Measuring tape, pencil, power drill, ⅛-inch drill bit, spade bit, safety eyewear

SHOPPING LIST: Peephole ($12.95)

TOTAL PRICE: $12.95

$50–$100/door, plus cost of the peephole

4

2. Wearing eye protection, drill a pilot hole with an ⅛-inch drill bit all the way through the door.

3. Attach a spade or "paddle" bit to your drill. The size will depend on the diameter of the peephole you purchased. Measure it and use the appropriate size.

4. Using the pilot hole as a guide, drill through the door with the paddle bit, stopping halfway. This is very important: *only drill halfway*! Drilling halfway from each side will prevent the door from splitting on the other side.

5. Move to the other side of the door, and drill from that side until you get all the way through to the hole you began on the other side.

6. Insert the viewer sleeve (this is the part of the peephole with the bubble) from the outside of the door.

7. Screw the other half of the viewer into the sleeve from the inside of the door.

8. Tighten the peephole by hand, with one hand on each side of the door.

- Make sure you center your drill hole *before* you start: measure across the door (horizontally) to be sure.
- When using the paddle bit, make sure the drill is level and straight. If you are off even just a tiny bit, you will have a hole that is not level.
- Many manufacturers say that you should take the door off its hinges for this project. I say—keep it on! In my opinion, taking the door off its hinges will not make installation easier. Keeping it on provides a stable way to hold the door in place.

Sliding Doors

Sliding doors need to be maintained, otherwise they become difficult to slide and can even jump off the tracks. The wheels on sliding doors glide along a track, much like the wheels of a train. The most important thing to remember is to keep the track *clean* and free of dirt and dust that can clog the wheels.

A good rule of thumb is to clean the tracks whenever you clean your floors. Vacuuming usually works best. Remember also to lubricate the tracks regularly. (There are dozens of inexpensive industrial and household lubricants on the market—ask your hardware salesperson.) A couple of times a year, it's also a good idea to clean the small drain holes on the sides of the tracks with a brush and soapy water. And every six months, it also pays to tighten the screws on the track, since loose screws will make the door drag and can also block the door's path. If your door needs to go higher or lower to run smoothly, adjust the screws on the side of the door.

FIXING SLIDING DOOR TRACKS

If your sliding door is still not gliding easily and/or closing snugly against the jamb, it's likely the rollers need more cleaning, or the track is bent. You might want to take the door off and try a simple tune-up.

Glass sliding doors are usually heavy and awkward, so it's best to have someone help you when you take it off its tracks. Worst-case scenario, trying to do it on your own could result in the door falling and shattering. When you do lay the door down, it's a good idea to have some kind of padding ready (old towels will do), to prevent scratching or damage to the rubber seals.

TUFF METER: 5  (because of how cumbersome the doors are—otherwise it's easy)

 TIMER: 30 minutes

 TUFF TOOLS: Hammer, screwdriver, block of wood

 SHOPPING LIST: Lubricant ($5.99)

TOTAL PRICE: $5.99 $30/door, plus materials

After cleaning tracks and rollers, you should oil only the rollers, not the tracks themselves because that can attract even more dirt.

How to fix sliding door tracks:

1. With one person on either side of the door, lift it up off its tracks and pull it away at the bottom. Then lower it from the upper track and place it gently on the floor. Lubricate and clean the rollers.

2. If an outside track is bent, place a block of wood on the track. Then take the hammer and bang the wood to straighten out the bend. Don't use your hammer directly on the track because that can cause more damage.

3. Once the tracks are straightened, replace the door. Slide the door shut, checking for an even gap between the door and the jamb as you do so.

4. Adjust the screws on the side of the door if needed to raise the door up or lower it down.

Sticky Door Latch or Bolt

We talked about a sticking door, but what if the door is fine and just the latch or bolt sticks? A sticking latch bolt is usually caused by a buildup of dirt and insufficient lubrication.

If your key sticks or has trouble turning, there is an easy way to fix it. Simply spray the keyhole with an all-purpose spray lubricant. Try the key again—it should work effortlessly.

If the latch bolt is misaligned with the strike plate, it won't fit into the strike plate's opening. Check the door for loose hinges first. If the problem persists, align the strike plate and latch bolt.

Warping, due to humidity or water penetration, is another cause of latch bolt problems. Use a straightedge to see if the door is warped, and straighten it if necessary.

ADJUSTING THE STRIKE PLATE

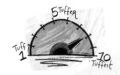

TUFF METER: 8

TIMER: 30 minutes

TUFF TOOLS: Pencil, screwdriver (chisel if needed)

SHOPPING LIST: Nothing

TOTAL PRICE: $0   **$20/door**

How to adjust or align your strike plate:

1. Unscrew the strike plate from the doorjamb and set it aside.

2. Take a pencil and mark up the end of bolt.

3. Close the door and turn the latch so that the bolt hits the doorjamb.

4. This should leave a mark on the doorjamb. This mark will show how you need to adjust the strike plate. You may need to use a chisel to adjust the hole.

5. Replace the strike plate so it aligns correctly with the bolt.

Repairing or Replacing a Doorknob

Just as new knobs can give a kitchen a brand-new look, doorknobs can really update the feel and look of your home. Are your doorknobs in good shape? Could they use a little updating? Are they loose or malfunctioning? If your doorknobs are dingy, you will be surprised at how simply changing them can really add to the look, feel, and cleanliness of your home.

Doorknobs are not too expensive and relatively easy to install. They come in a variety of shapes, sizes, colors, and locking mechanisms. If you are changing out an old doorknob, make sure your replacement is the same size. Most doorknobs are standard and interchangeable, but you want to make sure.

Essentially, you can approach replacing or fixing a doorknob in the same way. Typically, if your doorknob is loose or is in need of repair, you can simply replace the whole thing, or you can take it apart and tighten it up. Either way, the steps will be the same.

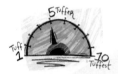

TUFF METER: 5

TIMER: 30 minutes

TUFF TOOLS: Pencil, screwdriver (chisel if needed)

SHOPPING LIST: Doorknob ($5.99 and up)

TOTAL PRICE: $5.99

$50/knob, plus materials

How to replace or fix a doorknob:

Out with the old:

1. Take the old doorknob out of the door by first removing the trim (the metal ring on the door surrounding the knob). Using a screwdriver, unscrew the two screws that hold the trim to the door. If the trim does not come off when you unscrew it, you may need to use a scraper or flat-head screwdriver to ease it off.

2. Next remove the two screws on either side of the doorknob mechanism. These are what holds the mechanism (and the two doorknobs) together.

3. Take a good look at how the doorknobs come apart. This will help when you install the new ones.

4. Take the old doorknobs out and set them aside.

5. You will be left with just the bolt (or the locking mechanism). Remove the two screws that hold this in the door, and remove the bolt.

6. Does the strike plate also need to be replaced? Take a look at it. If it's in good shape (and matches the color of the new doorknob) then keep it. If not, remove the two screws that hold it to the doorjamb and set it aside.

In with the new:

1. Take the bolt section and place it into the opening. Doorknob bolts have one side that is slanted. Make sure the slanted side faces the direction in which the door closes.

2. Screw in the bolt section with the screws provided.

3. You should have two doorknobs and two trims. Take the first trim and put it up to the door, covering the bolt section.

4. Take one of the doorknobs (the one with the mechanism that fits in the bolt—usually a square hole) and put it through the trim and the bolt.

5. Take the other doorknob and trim piece and put it on the other side of the door. Make sure you align these correctly. Remember the two long screws you took out of the old doorknob? Well, this one needs those too, so make sure they all line up.

6. Put in the long screws. Begin to tighten each just a little, going back and forth between both sides to make sure that the knob is coming together evenly.

7. You will now need to put the strike plate onto the doorjamb.

Strike plate:

1. Take a pencil and mark up the end of the bolt.

2. Close the door and turn the handle so that the bolt gently hits the doorjamb. Repeat this a few times.

3. This should leave a mark on the doorjamb. The mark will show you where you need to place the strike plate. You may need to use a chisel to adjust the previous hole.

4. Place the strike plate in the correct area, and attach it with the screws provided.

5. Test the lock a few times from both the inside and the outside to ensure that it has been assembled properly. Adjustments may need to be made.

6. If the strike plate seems loose, you may need to buy longer screws to get a tighter fit.

- When you take apart your old doorknob, keep all the pieces together or even reassemble them. Having this as a reference when you put in your new doorknob will be really helpful.
- Have patience. Doorknobs have a lot of tiny little pieces, which can disappear and cause confusion, so go slow. You'll do just fine!

Repairing or Replacing a Dead Bolt

We've seen it a million times on cop shows: the guys in uniform leap up the stairs, guns ready, and kick in the villain's front door.

If only the criminals had used longer screws!

Replacing an existing dead bolt, whether for extra security or because of a malfunction, is not a difficult job. Once you buy the lock, you can do the replacement in a few simple steps.

When you're preparing to put in a deadbolt, make sure you buy heavy-duty three-inch screws. In the real world, a person kicking in your door is more likely to be a thief than a police officer. Many dead bolts are mysteriously sold with small screws, which won't be enough to stop someone from kicking in your door without too much effort. (The same goes for an inside chain lock. Make sure you use long enough screws to prevent someone easily kicking in the door.)

There are two basic types of dead bolts: surface mount and internal. Surface mount deadbolts are easier to install, but internal deadbolts provide more security. You probably won't be surprised to hear that I recommend spending a little extra effort and money for the sake of your security: if you can, go for an internal dead bolt.

internal Deadbolt

surface mounted Deadbolt

Check to see if your door has a hole for a dead bolt. If not, you will need a hole saw for this project. Hole saws can be found at any hardware store. They are about the size of a measuring cup, with jagged teeth, and attach to a drill. Make sure the hole saw you buy matches the size of the new dead bolt.

REPLACING AN OLD DEAD BOLT

How to replace a dead bolt:

Out with the old:

1. Take the old dead bolt out of the door by using a screwdriver to remove the screws on the inside panel of the lock. Take a good look at how the lock comes apart. This will help when you are installing the new one.

2. Take the inside and outside pieces of the lock face and pull them apart and away from the door.

3. Remove the screws from the lock mechanism plate, which is located on the edge of the door.

4. Remove the screws from the strike plate, which is located on the doorjamb.

5. Measure the diameter of the hole in the door to be sure that you buy the same size dead bolt. Even better, you can take the old dead bolt to the hardware store to ensure that you buy the right size.

 Tuff Tip

Some models may be a bit more difficult to replace due to mounting brackets or slightly different assembly. The process of removing the old dead bolt can teach you things that make putting in the new unit that much easier, so remember the steps.

TIMER: 45 minutes

TUFF TOOLS: Screwdriver, tape measure (⅛-inch drill bit if needed)

SHOPPING LIST: New dead bolt ($27.99), screws (longer but the same diameter as the ones that come with your dead bolt, for the strike plate; $1.86–$4.07/box of 100)

TOTAL PRICE: $29.85 $50/door, plus materials

In with the new:

1. Place the new dead bolt mechanism in the hole in the door.

2. Instead of using the screws provided to attach the strike plate to the doorjamb, use longer screws that are the same diameter. This will make the lock much more secure. You may need to drill pilot holes first.

3. Put the inside and outside halves of the lock cylinder together. You can use the screws provided to attach them to each other and to the door.

4. Be sure that the bolt plate on the edge of the door is flush with the surface of the wood. Otherwise, it will keep the door from closing. If the new plate is slightly bigger than the space for the old plate, you may need to use a wood chisel to enlarge the area a bit.

5. Now attach the strike plate.

6. Take a pencil and mark up the end of the bolt.

7. Close the door and turn the latch so that the bolt gently hits the doorjamb. Repeat this a few times.

8. This should leave a mark on the doorjamb. The mark will show you where you need to place the strike plate. You may need to use a chisel to adjust the previous hole.

9. Place the strike plate in the correct spot, and attach it with the long screws, *not* the ones provided with the plate.

10. Test the lock a few times from both the inside and the outside to ensure that it has been assembled properly. Adjustments may need to be made.

INSTALLING A NEW DEAD BOLT

How to install a new dead bolt:

1. Buy a dead bolt and measure the diameter of the hole it will require you to make in the door. Buy a hole saw of the same size. The hole saw will attach directly to your drill.

> **SAFETY:** Wear eye protection whenever you are drilling into wood.

2. The dead bolt should be placed about 6 inches above the doorknob (from the center of the doorknob to the center of the dead bolt). Center it above the doorknob. Measure and mark this distance with a pencil.

3. Wearing eye protection, drill a pilot hole with an ⅛-inch drill bit all the way through the door in the very center of your mark.

4. Attach the hole saw to your drill.

5. Using the pilot hole as a guide, drill through the door, stopping halfway. Very important: *only drill halfway!* Drilling halfway from each side will prevent the door

from splitting. Make sure you hold your drill level and steady so that you do not create a crooked hole.

6. Move to the other side of the door, and drill from that side until you get all the way through with the hole saw. The hole saw will hold on to the drilled-out piece of the door. You can use a flat-head screwdriver to pry it out.

7. Place the new dead bolt mechanism into the hole of the door and follow steps 2–10 for replacing a dead bolt, on pages 126–127.

Installing a Doorstop

We've talked about drywall repair—by now, you *know* how to fix it. But let's talk about what we can do to prevent it. Sure, accidents happen, but one major reason we get holes in drywall is from our doorknobs banging into the wall. There is an easy way to combat this *before* it does any damage to your wall . . . install a doorstop!

TUFF METER: 2

TIMER: 15 minutes

TUFF TOOLS: Screwdriver, tape measure

SHOPPING LIST: Doorstop ($3.17 and up)

TOTAL PRICE: $3.17

$20/hour

How to install a doorstop:

The first order of business is to decide what type of doorstop you would like. A lot of it depends on what looks the best, since all makes and models will get the job done. There are three major types of doorstops:

1. **Baseboard-Mounted:** Spring-loaded or solid-shaft doorstops that attach to the baseboard

2. **Door Hinge–Mounted:** Solid-shaft doorstops that attach to the hinge of a door

3. **Wall-Mounted:** Rubber doorstops that attach to the wall where the knob comes in contact with the wall.

My favorite? The spring-loaded baseboard-mounted doorstop—it's easy to install, stays out of the way, doesn't break up the look of the wall, and makes a great "boing" noise when you hit it.

Baseboard-mounted doorstops:

1. Hold the door open gently against the wall.

2. Measure two inches in from the edge of the door. Mark this spot on the wall.

3. Follow the manufacturer's instructions. Usually, you will simply screw the doorstop directly into the baseboard. If it comes with separate screws, use those to attach it to the baseboard.

4. Make sure you are attaching to the baseboard and not the wall. If your wall is drywall and you attempt to attach the doorstop to that, you will push right through with one good swing of the door.

Door hinge–mounted:

1. This one, although not too difficult, requires a little more concentration and skill.

2. Grab a friend to hold the door.

3. Remove the pin of the hinge. If it gives you a little trouble, use the flat-head end of your screwdriver to pry it upward. Tap the screwdriver with a hammer for a little more force.

4. Put the hinge pin through the doorstop and through the door hinge, making sure the rubber sides face both the door and the wall.

5. Re-insert the pin through the entire hinge and voilà! Doorstop installed . . . and very sneaky. Usually, no one ever notices it is there.

Wall-mounted:

1. Open the door and set it gently against the wall.

2. Mark this *exact* spot on the wall.

3. Follow the manufacturer's instructions, but it should be easy to attach to the wall using the screw(s) provided.

4. If you are only screwing into drywall, use a wall anchor to make it more secure.

5

CABINETS

One way to give a kitchen or bathroom a new look is to replace the cabinets. But that can get really expensive, and I would *never* suggest you try to do that yourself. But don't fear—here is an easy (and much less expensive) way to go: replace the handles, knobs, hinges, and/or drawer pulls. It will give you a cleaner, more updated look without the big hit to the checkbook.

Most hardware stores have a comprehensive selection of knobs: little ball knobs, classic old-fashioned knobs, and little fun ones for kids (like hot-air balloons or animal shapes). There are endless creative options, and you can spend as little or as much as you want. As a rule of thumb: If it's got two screws, it's considered a handle. If it has one screw, it's considered a knob.

Replacing Cabinet Knobs, Handles, or Drawer Pulls

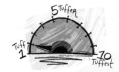

TUFF METER: 2

 TIMER: 10 minutes per knob

TUFF TOOLS: Screwdriver

 SHOPPING LIST: Handles, knobs, and/or drawer pulls ($3–$8)

 TOTAL PRICE: $3 $5–$10/knob or pull, plus materials

How to replace knobs or pulls:

1. Purchase knobs, handles, or drawer pulls that will match your current openings (i.e., the same number of screws in the same positions as what's already there).

2. Open the cabinet or drawer. While holding the knob in one hand, remove the screw from the interior with a screwdriver until loose enough to unscrew by hand. Check to see if it requires a flat-head or Phillips screwdriver.

3. Remove the old knob, handle, or pull.

4. The new knob, handle, or pull will come with its own screw(s). Place the screw(s) through the hole(s) from the inside.

5. Attach the knob, handle, or pull to the end of the screw and tighten by hand.

6. Use a screwdriver to make it tight.

Are your cabinet doors in need of some help? Other reasons cabinet doors can begin to look bad are that they are drooping, loosening, or sticking. Updating these small things may be just enough to give your kitchen or bathroom that new feel.

Sticky Cabinet Doors

How to fix sticky cabinet doors:

1. First locate the source of the problem. Where does the door stick? The easiest way to find out is to take a piece of carbon paper and put it between the edge of the door and the frame.

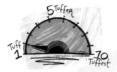

TUFF METER: 2

TIMER: 20 minutes

TUFF TOOLS: Trowel

SHOPPING LIST: Carbon paper ($5/50-pack), sandpaper ($1.89/6 sheets)

TOTAL PRICE: $6.89 $5/door

2. Open and close the door a few times so that the carbon leaves its mark on the frame. Where it leaves its mark is your trouble spot!

3. Sand down the trouble spot until the mark from the carbon paper is no longer visible.

4. Do the carbon paper test along all edges that are giving you trouble, and repeat the process until all the doors close smoothly.

Loose Hinges

When cabinet doors don't hang straight or open smoothly, tighten the screws on the hinges. If the screw holes are worn and the wood won't hold the screws tight, you can make the following simple repair.

How to repair loose hinges:

1. Remove the cabinet door by unscrewing the hinges from the door.

TIMER: 1 hour

TUFF TOOLS: Putty knife, drill

SHOPPING LIST: Wood putty (powdered; $2.17), dowel (¼-inch; $11.99/twelve), wood glue ($3.75)

TOTAL PRICE: $17.91 $5/hinge, plus materials

2. Unscrew the hinges from the face frame.

3. Find a wooden dowel with the same diameter as the screw hole—a golf tee often works. I also have used a toothpick. Especially for smaller screw holes, a toothpick will provide just enough grasp to hold the hinge in place.

4. Coat the end of the dowel, golf tee, or toothpick with wood glue and insert it into the hole.

5. Reattach the hinge and door.

 Tuff Tip

You can make the same repair to the screw holes in the door, but take care not to drill through the door.

Repairing Drawers

If your drawers are giving you trouble, there could be several things at fault. Your first job is to figure out what's going on. Is your drawer pull or handle loose? Does your drawer fall off the track? Is it hard to open? Is it difficult to slide? Will it not close all the way?

DRAWER PULLS

If your loose drawer pulls will not tighten with a screwdriver, you may need to bring in some reinforcements.

TUFF METER: 4

TIMER: 30 minutes

TUFF TOOLS: Putty knife, drill, screwdriver, sandpaper

SHOPPING LIST: Wood putty (powdered; $2.17)

TOTAL PRICE: $2.17

$1/pull

How to tighten loose drawer pulls:

1. Tighten loose drawer pulls or handles by filling the worn screw holes with wood putty. Use a powdered putty that you mix with water just before applying; this type of putty tends to dry harder than most premixed products.

2. Remove the drawer pull's screw, and make sure there's no dust or grime in the screw hole. Mix the putty to the proper consistency, and firmly pack some into the hole with a putty knife.

3. Wipe off any excess putty with a damp cloth.

4. When the putty has dried, drill a pilot hole. In this case, you would want to use a drill bit that is the same size as the screw. This should make the area tight and provide a solid base for your drawer pull.

5. Reattach the drawer pull or handle using the directions above.

DRAWERS OFF THE TRACK

How to repair drawers that have fallen off the track:

2

1. Take out the drawer and set it aside.

2. Look at the tracks. Many metal tracks often get bent or misshaped. There is an easy way to combat this. Take a small piece of wood and place it behind the track. Use screws to hold it in place.

3. This should straighten out the track. Play around with different-sized pieces of scrap wood until you find a piece that makes the track parallel to the drawer.

TUFF METER: 5

 TIMER: 15 minutes

 TUFF TOOLS: Screwdriver, scrap wood pieces

 SHOPPING LIST: Carbon paper ($5/50-pack), sandpaper ($1.89/6 sheets)

TOTAL PRICE: $6.89   **$20/hour**

HARD-TO-OPEN DRAWERS

If you have a drawer that is hard to open, before going all the way and deciding to replace the tracks, remove the drawer, clean the tracks and rollers, and lubricate the rollers. This may fix the problem.

Sometimes drawers stick because of humidity. Since wood tends to shrink and swell in response to the weather, you may simply need to "dry out" your drawer. Take out the drawer and store it in a warm, dry place for forty-eight hours. Then replace it. You can sand any places that still stick. This may fix your problem. To prevent the drawer from swelling again, you can coat it with clear wood sealer or polyurethane.

If your drawer has wooden tracks, take out the drawer, and clean both the drawer and the tracks with a damp rag. You can sand down all contact areas with 100-grit sandpaper to remove any grime. Then spray the tracks with furniture polish. The wax in the polish should make the drawer slide much easier.

Do you have drawers that droop? Wooden drawers that have worn away over time will tend to droop in the front. There is a *very* simple way to take care of this problem. Take thumbtacks and place them in the bottom corners of the opening. This will provide a nonfriction surface that will both lift the drawer and cut down on future wear.

REPLACING DRAWER TRACKS

If you have tried all of the tricks above and find that your drawer is still difficult to open, the rollers and/or tracks may need to be replaced or adjusted. Bottom mount rollers are the easiest to install. Make sure the new drawer guides (tracks) are no longer than the length of the drawer, measuring from the rear to the back of the drawer face.

TUFF METER: 7

TIMER: 1 hour

TUFF TOOLS: Drill, tape measure, level

SHOPPING LIST: Drawer tracks (roller kit; $4.19/2), wood screws ($1.86–$4.07/100)

TOTAL PRICE: $6.05 $30–$50/hour

3

6

How to replace drawer tracks:

1. Remove the drawer and unscrew the old track from the cabinet.

2. The manufacturer of the new tracks will give you a diagram. Follow their instructions.

3. First measure where the track will fit onto the cabinet. Mark this so that it is easy to find when you put the track in place.

4. Align the top and front edges of the track with the marks. Use the screws provided to fasten the track to the side of the cabinet. Do one side first. Then level the track from front to back and secure the other side with a screw.

5. Follow the same procedure for the second track on the other side.

6. Unscrew the old drawer guides from the drawer.

7. Set the new guides in place with the wheels toward the rear. Make sure that the front edge of the guide is flush with the back of the drawer face. Attach using the screws provided.

8. Insert the drawer into the cabinet by placing the rollers in the corresponding places in the tracks.

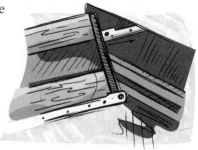

8

6

OUTDOOR

Gutters

CLEANING GUTTERS

Keeping gutters clean is a task that is so often over-looked—and yet so important. Why? Because of Mother Nature's gifts of rain and fire.

The first—rain—is obvious: when it rains heavily, blocked guttres will overflow in all the places you don't want them to. The kind of damage this can do in even a short amount of time is remarkable. Water leaking onto roofs and down walls can cause thousands of dollars worth of damage. Over the long term, mold is a potential problem that's not just smelly, but dangerous to you and your family's health, and again, it can cost thousands of dollars to eradicate once it gets going.

The second reason to clean your gutters is that it just might save your life—especially if your property backs onto a park or woodland. Even if you're a city dweller, gutters full of dried leaves are a tinderbox waiting to ignite. Dried leaves will accelerate the pace of any fire and could make the difference between saving your house, other people's houses, and even lives.

So clean your drains—it's easy and can save thousands. Do it twice a year at least. A leaf blower is an easy way to go. You can also use a hose, though you have to decide if wasting a bunch of water is less environmentally friendly then running a motor. Use a trowel to remove leaves, twigs, and

Don't have a trowel? Try cutting a rectangular motor-oil container into a scoop. It is just the right size and fits into your hand perfectly.

- If there is a clog in the downspout, try prying it free with the handle of a broom. Test with water from a hose. If you still have a clog, try some homemade water pressure. Try wrapping a large rag around the hose and placing it in the opening at the top of the downspout. The rag should be packed in firmly so the water is forced down the spout. Hold it firmly in place and get someone else to turn on the tap full force. This should break up the clog and get the water flowing freely.

- You can go a step further and shield gutters with mesh gutter guards to prevent future clogs.

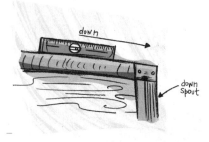

other debris. Be sure to use a ladder and climb up to check the full length of the gutters. Just one little spot left uncleaned can result in a backup.

Keep gutters and downspouts clean so that rain falling on the roof is directed well away from the foundation. Almost all wet-basement problems are the direct result of water collecting near the foundation of a house, a situation often caused by clogged and overflowing gutters and downspouts.

Check the slope of gutters with a level, and adjust them, if necessary. Gutters should angle toward the downspouts so water flows freely rather than hanging out in the gutters and encouraging buildup and rust.

Test your cleanup job. You must waste a bit of water to test your gutters and downspouts. But don't worry . . . wasting a little now will help you *save* a lot more in the future. Put a hose at the top corner of your gutter and make sure that the water flows freely down the downspout.

PATCHING LEAKS

If you have minor leaks in your gutters, you can use a gutter patching kit to make temporary repairs. However, if there is a big leak or a lot of damage, you will need to replace the entire section of gutter. Read the manufacturer's recommendations and directions before purchasing a gutter repair kit. Grab the one that makes the most sense for the climate you live in, and follow the directions.

Stucco

TUFF CHIX DICTIONARY

Stucco is a durable finish for exterior walls, usually composed of cement, sand, and lime, and applied while wet. (It can also refer to some types of plaster or cement finish for interior walls and interior wall ornamentation, such as moldings.)

PATCHING A SMALL AREA OF STUCCO

This simple repair method works well for damaged areas that are less than two square feet. For more extensive damage, the stucco will have to be removed all the way to the wall surface and rebuilt in layers. (Follow the steps in the project after this one.)

Matching the texture and color is the trickiest part of stucco repair. Stucco comes in many different finishes. The best thing to do is play around with the finish, be creative, and keep playing until you get the best match.

SAFETY: For larger repairs in particular, wear safety glasses and a particle mask or respirator when cutting stucco.

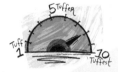

TUFF METER: 8

 TIMER: 1 hour

TUFF TOOLS: Wire brush, putty knife (or trowel), whisk broom

 SHOPPING LIST: Metal primer ($29.99), bonding adhesive ($2.99), premixed stucco ($9.99/gallon), masonry paint ($29.99)

TOTAL PRICE: $72.96

$20–$30/hour, plus materials

How to patch a small area of stucco:

1. Begin by removing any loose material with a wire brush. Use the hammer and chisel or a knife to undercut the stucco surrounding the damaged area so that the patch will be securely locked in.

2. Use the brush to clean rust from any exposed wall and to remove any stucco knocked loose in undercutting. Also make sure the surface is free of all dust and dirt.

3. Paint the broken edges of the stucco with bonding adhesive, which will improve the bond between the old stucco and the stucco patch. (Another option is to thoroughly wet down the damaged area and keep it damp for 12 hours before patching to prevent the moisture from being drawn too quickly from the patch and weakening it.)

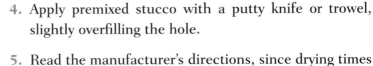

4. Apply premixed stucco with a putty knife or trowel, slightly overfilling the hole.

5. Read the manufacturer's directions, since drying times vary. Feather the edges until the patch blends into the surrounding surface.

6. Use a whisk broom, washcloth, or trowel to duplicate the original texture. This is probably the most difficult part of the project, but don't despair! Have patience and keep playing around until you get the texture you are looking for. Let the patch dry for several days, then touch it up with masonry paint, matching the color to the rest of the stucco.

REPAIRING A LARGE AREA OF STUCCO

Typically, Mother Nature will cause most of the damage to stucco, but this damage is usually small cracks. Larger damage is usually caused by us—tripping with a ladder, getting the car too close, all of those pesky accidents that we later curse ourselves about. Duplicating stucco textures takes patience, skill, and experience, so it's a good idea to practice before taking on a major repair. This might be a great project to hire a professional (HAP).

TUFF METER: 10

TIMER: 1 hour + dry time. Total: 1 week.

TUFF TOOLS: Drill, hammer, masonry chisel, tin snips, mortar box, spray bottle, trowel, safety glasses

SHOPPING LIST: Particle mask ($2.99), self-turning metal lath, roofing nails ($4.99), sand ($3.99/bag), portland cement ($7.38/bag), masonry cement ($14.94), finish-coat stucco mix ($9.99)

TOTAL PRICE: $44.28

$20–$30/hour, plus materials

How to repair a large area of stucco:

1. Remove the old stucco by making a starter hole with a drill and a masonry bit, then using a masonry chisel and hammer to chip away all the stucco in the repair area.

2. Cut the self-turning metal lath, which looks like a metal screen. Ask your hardware store personnel to help you find it. Attach it to the sheathing with roofing nails. If it takes more than one width of lath, overlap

2

4

5

the pieces by 2 inches. If the patch extends to the base of the wall, attach a metal stop bead at the bottom so the stucco can't leak out.

3. Premixed stucco works well for small jobs, but for large ones, it's more economical to mix your own. Combine three parts sand, two parts portland cement, and one part masonry cement. Add just enough water so the mixture holds its shape when squeezed. Mix only as much as you can use in about an hour.

4. Apply a ⅜-inch thick layer of stucco directly to the metal lath. Push the stucco into the mesh until it fills the gap between the mesh and the sheathing. Important: Don't fill the hole completely—you will need to apply two more layers after the first one has cured.

5. Score horizontal grooves into the wet surface.

6. Let the stucco dry for two days, misting it with water every 2 to 4 hours to help it cure evenly.

7. Apply a second, smooth layer of stucco. Build up the stucco to within ¼ inch of the original surface. Let the patch dry for two days, misting as before.

8. Combine finish-coat stucco mix with just enough water for the mixture to hold its shape.

9. Dampen the patch area, then apply the finish coat to match the original surface. The finish coat was dabbed on with a whisk broom then flattened with a trowel. Dampen the patch periodically for a week. Let it dry for several more days before painting it.

Painting Exterior Walls

TUFF CHIX DICTIONARY

An exterior wall is any wall located on the outside of your home. It is usually covered by a surface such as stucco, wood siding, vinyl siding, or other outdoor material.

Exterior painting is quite a challenge, yet if you decide to tackle this project, you will make a lasting change for the better to your home. It can make a dramatic difference and even extend the life of your home. If you do it yourself, you will save thousands of dollars. Buy the best paint. High-quality paint lasts longer and will typically cover better and be easier to apply.

TUFF METER: 4

TIMER: Depends on how much you have to paint, but a normal 10 x 10-foot wall should take you about 1 hour, with 2 hours of preparation time of the exterior wall.

TUFF TOOLS: Paint roller frame

SHOPPING LIST: Heavy-duty (nap) roller cover ($1.99–$9.99); paint ($12.99 and up)

TOTAL PRICE: $14.98 $30–$40/hour, plus paint

Tuff Tips

- Have you ever tried to paint your fingernails outside, ladies? It's no fun. The sun will make the polish dry too quickly, and the wind will usually blow unwanted debris or gnats into your masterpiece. Well, painting the outside of your home is no different. Try not to paint in direct sunlight because the paint will dry too quickly, leaving streaks and lines that will give away that you attempted to try this without a professional.

- Time your painting project to take advantage of shade during the day. Make sure it's not too windy, so nothing sticks to your paint job. It is always best to paint in temperatures above fifty degrees—so you might want to wait for summer. There are certain paints that are formulated for cold-weather application, but they are more expensive and harder to work with. If you can wait, you will be happy you did.

PREPARING EXTERIOR WALLS

Just as with interior painting, preparation is very important. Here is the best way to prepare your home for a professional-looking paint job.

TUFF METER: 3

TIMER: Depends on how much you have to paint and the condition of the wall. Estimate about 2 hours of prep time for a typical exterior wall of 10 x 10 feet.

TUFF TOOLS: Drop cloths (sheets or canvas), heat gun, putty knife, sandpaper (100 grit or similar), siding sander, wire brush, screwdriver (both Phillips and flat), scraper

SHOPPING LIST: Blue painter's tape ($5.59), joint compound ($4.99) or wall putty

TOTAL PRICE: $10.58

$20/hour, plus materials

How to prepare exterior walls:

1. Scrape off all flaking or loose sections of paint with a wire brush or putty knife.

2. Fill any holes and caulk any joints (see the sections on patching wood, vinyl, and aluminum siding later in this chapter). Sand to match texture.

3. Remove any hinges, shutters, light fixtures, or anything you do not want painted—and that will come off.

4. Cover any trees, bushes, decks, foundations, and grass. When you are covering living things, use only breathable cloths such as sheets or canvas. Do not use plastic.

5. Clean the house. You can do this by hosing it down, taking a broom to debris and cobwebs, and clearing the brush around your house.

6. Patch and prime any sections of untreated wood.

PAINT REMOVAL

Removing old paint is a lot easier when you use the right tools for each task.

Use a heat gun to loosen thick layers of old paint. Aim the gun at the surface and scrape the paint as soon as it releases. To remove large areas of paint on wood siding, use a hand sander with a disk that's as wide as the reveal on your siding. To remove loose paint and rust from metal hardware, use a wire brush. Apply metal primer immediately to prevent new rust. To scuff metal siding and trim, use medium-coarse steel wool or a coarse abrasive pad. Wash the surface before priming and painting.

Pressure washing is one of the most efficient methods of cleaning and removing loose paint from an exterior. Allow all surfaces to dry thoroughly before continuing with preparation work. Since pressure washing won't remove all the loose paint, the next step is to scrape the surface with a scraper or sandpaper. Be careful not to damage the surface with overly aggressive scraping. Use detail scrapers to remove loose paint in hard-to-reach areas. Some of these scrapers have interchangeable heads that match common trim profiles. Smooth out rough paint with a finishing sander and 80-grit sandpaper. Use sanding blocks and 80- to 120-grit sandpaper to sand hard-to-reach areas of trim. Sanding blocks are available in a variety of shapes and sizes, including, for instance, a teardrop design. Or, you can make sanding blocks from dowels, wood scraps, garden hose, or other household materials: just wrap sandpaper around them. Cut old sanding strips to sand small, detailed areas of trim.

Inspect all surfaces for cracks, rot, and other damage. Mark affected areas with colored pushpins or tape. Fill holes and cracks with epoxy wood filler.

Use a finishing sander with 120-grit sandpaper to sand down repaired areas, as well as ridges and hard edges left from the scraping process, creating a smooth surface.

WHAT SHOULD YOU PAINT FIRST?

There are two main sections of your home that need exterior paint: the walls and the trim. (The trim includes all the details found around windows, doors, soffits, fasciae, corner boards, etc.) You will want to paint all the trim first. That way, if you should get any of the trim paint on the house, you can easily cover it when you paint the walls. Next, paint the walls, from top to bottom.

PREPARING TRIM SURFACES

How to prepare trim surfaces:

1. Scuff-sand glossy surfaces on doors, window casings, and any surface painted with enamel paint. Use 100-grit sandpaper.

2. Fill any cracks in the siding or gaps around windows and door trim with paintable siliconized acrylic caulk (see the sections on patching siding later in this chapter).

3. Remove clear finishes: clear topcoats and sealants can flake and peel, just like paint. Pressure wash any stained or unpainted surfaces that have been treated with a wood preservative or protectant, before recoating them with fresh sealant.

4. Use a stiff-bristled brush to dislodge any flakes of loosened surface coating that weren't removed by pressure washing. Don't use a wire brush on wood surfaces.

5. Remove rust and loose paint from metal hardware, such as railings and ornate trim, with a wire brush. Cover the surface with metal primer immediately after brushing to prevent the formation of new rust.

Tutt Tip

Dissolve rust on metal hardware with a diluted muriatic acid solution. When working with muriatic acid, it's important to wear safety equipment, work in a well-ventilated area, and follow all directions and precautions.

6. Scuff-sand metal siding and trim with medium-coarse steel wool or a coarse abrasive pad. Wash the surface before priming and painting.

7. Remove loose mortar, mineral deposits, or paint from mortar lines (grout) in masonry surfaces with a drill and wire-wheel attachment. Clean broad, flat surfaces with a wire brush.

8. Correct any minor damage with masonry repair products before repainting.

PRIMING EXTERIORS

Priming exteriors is just like priming interiors, and just as important. Use the following chart to help you with preparation and the types of primer to use.

Wood Siding

horizontal wood siding

shingles + shakes

These days, wood siding is almost always chosen for aesthetic reasons—it looks good and it feels warm. The key to wood siding is maintenance, maintenance, and more maintenance.

Well-maintained wood siding can last several decades, and beyond, if it is well cared for. There are two main categories of wood siding: clapboard and other "milled board" siding (yep, that just means wood processed through a mill), which is usually laid horizontally; and shingles and shakes, which are small sections of wood laid next to one another and overlapped.

PATCHING AND REPAIR

Wood siding should be hard all the way through. If you have dry rot (a fungus that makes wood crumbly) or insect damage in your exterior (or interior) wood siding, there's no way

SURFACE TYPE TO BE PAINTED	PREPARATION	TYPE OF PRIMER
Unpainted wood	• Sand wood first with a rough paper and then with a smooth paper to create a smooth and porous surface • Use a damp cloth to remove any excess dirt or dust particles • Apply primer	Exerior latex primer for exterior use, interior latex primer for interior use
Previously painted wood	• Wipe down the wood with a wet cloth, using both soap and water • Rinse wood thoroughly with water • Let dry completely • Take 150-grit sandpaper and sand wood lightly, not to remove paint, but to make a porous surface • Gently scrape off any loose paint chips and sand again if necessary • Use a damp cloth to remove any excess dirt or dust particles • Apply primer	Latex primer, but keep in mind that the painted wood is already primed. Use primer only on bare wood that may have presented itself during the scraping and sanding process Exterior latex primer for exterior use, interior latex primer for interior use
Previously varnished wood	• Wipe down the wood with a wet cloth, using soap and water • Rinse wood thoroughly with water • Let dry thoroughly • Take 150-grit sandpaper and sand wood lightly, to remove glossy surface • Use a damp cloth to remove any excess dirt or dust particles • Apply primer	Exterior latex primer for exterior use, interior latex primer for interior use
Unpainted walls or drywall	• Use a damp cloth to remove any dirt or dust particles • Apply primer	Interior flat latex primer

SURFACE TYPE TO BE PAINTED	PREPARATION	TYPE OF PRIMER
Previously painted walls or drywall	• Wipe down the wood with a damp cloth, using soap and water • Fill in any holes with putty (see "Drywall Repair," p. 40) • Let dry thoroughly • Apply primer, if necessary	Interior flat latex primer, but only if you are painting over dark colors: otherwise, there is no need for primer
Unpainted plaster	• Use a damp cloth to remove any dirt or dust particles • Apply primer	Interior flat latex primer or polyvinyl acrylic primer.
Previously painted plaster	• Wipe down the wood with a damp cloth, using soap and water. • Fill in any holes with putty (see fixing section) • Let dry thoroughly • Apply primer if necessary	Interior flat latex primer or using soap and water you are painting over dark colors

Tuff Tip

You can use oil-based primer for any of these applications, however, I do not recommend it. It is harder to clean up, takes longer to dry, and smells bad.

around it. You'll have to replace it. And you *must* replace it. It will just lead to more damage if you don't.

You can test for rot (and termites) by pushing the eraser end of a pencil or any hard object into the wood boards. If any are soft and your pencil pushes through them, they need repairing. You might be able to get away with a patch repair, rather than replacing one or more whole boards. Either way, repairing simple problems as soon as you discover them will prevent the wood from deteriorating. Simple repairs to damaged wood siding include fixing split boards, filling holes, and repainting.

- Before you start repairs or painting, make sure you have determined the cause of the problem. A warped board might be the result of a clogged drainpipe. You should fix this *before* you start thinking about repairs or replacement boards. Similarly, soft wood might be the result of termites. If this is the case, you will need to call a pest-control professional or risk further serious structural damage to your house.
- All wood siding and repaired wood pieces should be sealed, stained, or painted for protection from decay, insects, and weathering.

Shingles and shakes are small enough to replace rather than repair, assuming you can find good matches for them.

FIXING SPLIT BOARDS

When most people see a cracked board, they think they need to take the entire board off and replace it. If the wood is in good condition, then all you simply need to do is repair it.

TUFF METER: 5

TIMER: 45 minutes

TUFF TOOLS: Chisel, hammer

SHOPPING LIST: Waterproof glue ($3.75), nails or screws ($1.86–$4.07/100), sandpaper ($1.89/6 sheets)

TOTAL PRICE: $7.50

$20/hour, plus materials

How to fix split boards:

1. Pry the sides of the crack apart slightly, and run the sandpaper along both sides of the entire crack. This gets the wood ready to receive the glue. Remember buffing your nails, ladies, to receive the nail polish? This is the same idea.

2. Coat the edges of the board with waterproof glue.

3. Nail or screw the board into position, or if the repair is in a very visible location, drive nails just below the board to hold it in place as the glue dries.

4. Wipe off any excess glue with a damp washcloth.

5. Wait several days, to make sure it is dry, and remove the nails.

REPAINTING

If paint problems such as blistering or peeling are confined to a small area, you can touch them up. If they are more extensive, you may want to repaint the entire wall or house. Again, before painting, *solve the cause of the problem*.

Also before painting, make sure the surfaces are clean, dry, and hard. Don't ignore soft spots, which may indicate fungus or termites.

Wait until you have warm weather. It's best to paint in dry weather with temperatures between fifty and ninety degrees. This will give you a much better finish, and you will be happier with your work. So if you can wait, wait.

How to repaint wood siding:

1. Make sure the area is completely clean and dry. If you need to clean it, wait 24 hours before attempting to paint to be sure that the area is dry.

TUFF METER: 3

TIMER: The time will depend on the area that needs to be repainted and the condition of the wood. A 2-foot section should take approximately 45 minutes.

TUFF TOOLS: You can use an electric hand sander or just do it by hand.

SHOPPING LIST: 65-grit and 100-grit sandpaper ($1.89–$2.49), paint ($12.99 and up)

TOTAL PRICE: $17.37

$25–$30/hour, plus materials

2. Take the 65-grit sandpaper and sand away any area that has bubbled or peeled.

3. Take the 100-grit sandpaper and run over that same area to make a smoother surface.

4. Wipe the area down with a lightly dampened cloth.

5. Apply paint.

REPLACING A BOARD

To replace a milled board, you'll need to find a new piece that is exactly the same pattern as the original. Finding boards to match older patterns isn't always easy. An alternative option is to take a piece from a less conspicuous part of your house. Sure, you will have to replace that one as well, but if it's not a perfect match, your guests will be less likely to see it. The more expensive option is to have new pieces custom milled.

TUFF METER: 7

TIMER: 2 hours

TUFF TOOLS: Hammer, circular saw

SHOPPING LIST: Roofing cement (only if roofing paper is damaged; $19.99–$24.99), paint ($12.99 and up)

TOTAL PRICE: $32.93

$50–$60/board or
$20–$30/hour

2

How to replace a board:

1. Pull out any exposed nails with a hammer.

2. Cut out the damaged area with a circular saw after you have pulled out all of the exposed nails. Be *very* careful not to saw through the underlying paper. If the damaged area is big enough, you can simply remove the entire board and leave the circular saw in the toolshed.

3. I told you not to, but just in case you have damaged the underlying paper, repair it with roofing cement.

4. Measure the piece of wood siding you removed.

5. Cut a new piece to the exact same size.

Tuff Tip

It might be easier to paint the board *before* you put it into place. That way, it will be all ready to go once you nail it into place. This also keeps the area around the board paint free.

6. Nail in the new piece of board so that it fits in snugly in the open area.

7. Caulk any nail holes, wiping off any excess caulking.

8. Paint to match.

Vinyl Siding

Vinyl siding's popularity today reflects its ease of maintenance. Vinyl siding is made of polyvinyl chloride—a strong, impact-resistant, rigid material that is replacing metal in a lot of new construction.

The texture of vinyl siding resembles wood and comes in a huge range of styles and colors. Unlike wood siding, it's not susceptible to rot and termites, it's waterproof, and it *never* needs to be painted. No wonder it's the number one siding material on the market. Low maintenance!

TUFF METER: 9

TIMER: 1 hour

TUFF TOOLS: Flat-head screwdriver, aviation snips (tin snips)

SHOPPING LIST: Vinyl siding ($3.97/sq. ft.)

TOTAL PRICE: $3.97/sq. ft.

$20–$30/hour

How to repair vinyl siding:

1. Starting at the seam nearest the damaged area, unlock the interlocking joints, using a flat-head screwdriver. Install spacers—the same as used with tile—then remove the fasteners on the top piece of damaged siding.

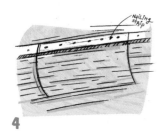

2. Cut out the damaged area, using aviation snips (tin snips). This may sound difficult, but it's actually not. You snip the area just like you would cut through a piece of thick fabric.

3. Cut a replacement piece that is 4 inches longer than the open area.

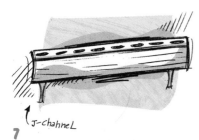

4. Trim off 2 inches of the nailing strip from each end of the overlap area.

5. Slide the piece into position. Put ring-shank siding nails (a big flat-head nail) in the nailing strip.

6. Drive the nails in with a hammer.

7. Slip the J-channel (thing that you hang the siding on) over the nailing strip.

How to patch aluminum siding:

1. Cut out the damaged area with aviation snips. Leave an exposed area on top of the uppermost piece to act as a bonding surface.

2. Cut a patch 4 inches wider than the repair area, then remove the nailing strip from the piece.

3. Smooth the edges with metal sandpaper.

TUFF METER: 9

TIMER: 1 hour

TUFF TOOLS: Aviation snips

SHOPPING LIST: Metal sandpaper ($2.49), roofing cement ($19.99–$24.99)

TOTAL PRICE: $22.48

$20–$30/hour, plus materials

4. Nail the lower patches in place by driving ring-shank siding nails through the nailing strips, starting with the lowest piece.

5. Apply roofing cement to the back of the top piece, tl press it into place, slipping the J-channel over the n ing strip below.

6. Caulk the seams.

cement glue on back

5

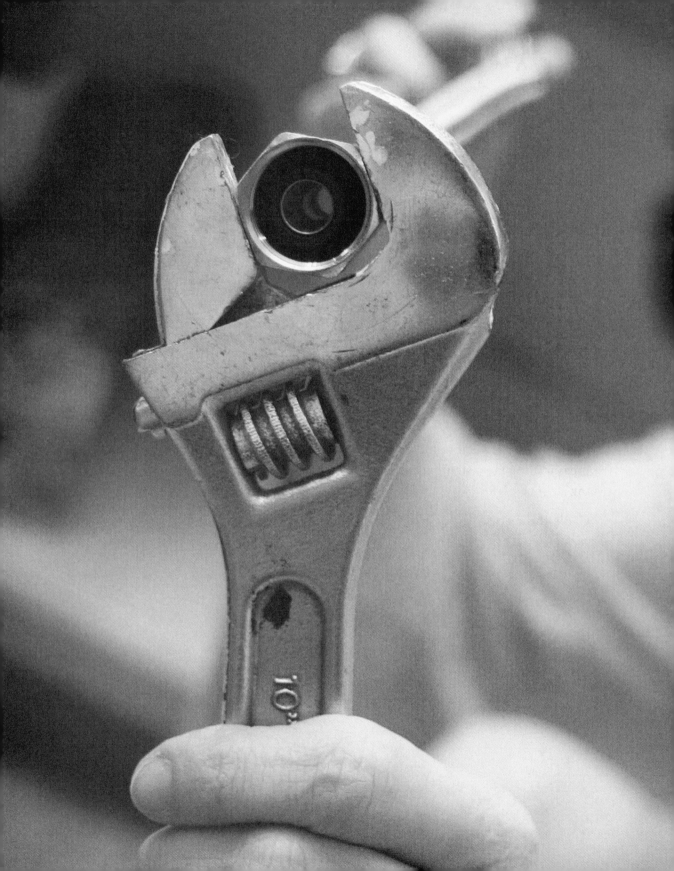

PLUMBING

Plumbing, like electrical repairs, is one of those tasks that I ran from. I was so frightened by the possibility of doing something wrong, springing a leak, and flooding my house. Or even worse, creating an annoying little drip that would haunt me for weeks. I have seen gushing fire hydrants in the street, and that is what I pictured my indoor pipes looking like if I tried to fix my backed-up sink or my malfunctioning toilet.

Plumbers are expensive and can often be avoided altogether. But plumbers do have their place in this world, and I love them for it. As you read on, keep in mind that this is not a comprehensive guide to fixing your plumbing problems— just the ones that you can tackle easily and confidently. Keep that plumber's number handy for when you encounter a *big* plumbing job.

One thing you can do to help, even when the big problems strikes, is to learn how to shut off your water supply at the valves!

Valves

Valves make it possible to shut off water at many points in the system. If a pipe breaks or a plumbing fixture begins to leak, the valve allows you to shut off the water to the damaged area until it's repaired. Valves can be your best friend when you have a leak. All you need to do is crank them clockwise to shut off the water supply (lefty-loosey, righty-tighty).

Although replacing valves is a bit more intense, and may require you to HAP, I want you to be familiar with what you have in your home. Since several types of valves are commonly found in homes, I have listed them below. When a good valve goes bad, I want you to be able to head down to the hardware store knowing the correct term or to tell your plumber exactly what you need done.

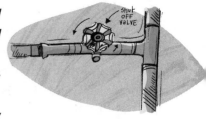

TUFF CHIX DICTIONARY

Shutoff valves: These are the most common valves you will come in contact with. They control water to a single fixture. You will find these below sinks and toilets, behind washing machines, etc.

Saddle valves: These are small fittings you will find connecting a re-frigerator, icemaker, or sink-mounted water filter to a copper water pipe.

Hose bib valves: These are often used to connect rubber utility hoses and appliance hoses to a water supply. They are smaller in nature.

Gate valves: Gate valves do just what they sound like they might do: control the water flow by rais-ing and lowering a "gate." They either allow water flow or stop the flow completely. You will not typically see these in highly visible areas around the home. They screw down into place when closed, and screw up when open.

Globe valves: These have a curved chamber and are named for their globelike (spherical) body shape. They operate by screwing a handwheel, and are used in applications where frequent operation is required.

Blocked or Overflowing Drains

You'd be amazed by what people will put down their drains. Here's the deal: even when you have a garbage disposal, you should put the *absolute minimum* of everything besides non-toxic, soluble liquids down your drain.

We girls (and a handful of you guys) with gorgeous long, flowing locks are all too familiar with clogged bath and shower drains. Short of getting a crew cut, blocked bathroom drains can be hard to avoid. Getting a fine drain cover defi-nitely helps, though this is not always possible for old or smaller drains.

Common sense, on the other hand, can be used avoid most blockages in kitchen sinks, and especially in garbage dis-posals. Just because you have a disposal unit, doesn't mean you should put as much garbage as possible in it! Small

amounts of organic food scraps are okay. Pretty much every-thing else should be avoided; rice and pasta are particularly common causes of garbage disposals gone wrong. Other items to stay away from are carrot and potato peels. It's tempt-ing when peeling these vegetables to just push the skins down the drain, but refrain! It will save your pipes.

I had a tenant once who repeatedly called about a kitchen sink backup. Although the garbage disposal worked fine, it was *what* he was putting down the sink that was the problem: rice—and lots of it. Sure it was soft and went down fairly easy, but it was sticky and would collect on the side of the pipes.

Chemical Treatments

Chemical treatments are usually the easiest way to unclog a drain, but they are not environmentally friendly. Remember, whatever you put down your sink eventually flows into the sea. Also, be extra careful not to splash these chemicals onto your skin, and be especially wary of getting them in your eyes.

There is a huge range of chemical drain uncloggers avail-able from supermarkets and hardware stores, in both liquid and solid form. Read the instructions carefully because the products vary. The general procedure, however, is to pour the chemical into the drain, wait for it to dissolve the blockage, and flush the drain with running water. If the blockage doesn't clear after a couple of tries, prepare yourselves, ladies, for the snake!

Tuff Tip

Some chemicals will discolor drain fittings, and they can damage the plastic or rubber parts of a garbage disposal. Again, avoid this by carefully reading the package of each individual treatment.

Sink Snakes

A sewer snake, or auger, is a handy tool to have around the house. It's basically a flexible metal rod with a spiral hook or ball at the end, which is long enough to reach deep into a drainpipe. A snake enables you to break up a clog, allowing it to be flushed down through the pipes. It also enables you to grip onto a clog and pull it out.

TUFF CHIX DICTIONARY

There are two basic types of snakes. Most common is the drain snake, which is a coiled rod or flattened metal strip. It comes in a variety of different lengths. The closet snake has a bent tip made to fit into a toilet's in-trap. Some drain snakes fit on an attachment to an electric drill, giving you more power to force through a clog.

TUFF METER: 4

TIMER: 10 minutes (if you find the clog)

TUFF TOOLS: Closet snake or drain snake

SHOPPING LIST: Nothing, unless you need to buy the snake. Most likely, someone in your neighborhood will have one you can borrow.

TOTAL PRICE: $0 $65–$125

How to clear a clogged sink with a snake:

1. Push the snake into the drain. When the coil hits an obstruction, turn the handle and ram the snake into the clog. Sometimes that's all it takes to clear the line, spinning the clog away or chopping it up.

2. If the pipe is still blocked, crank the rod clockwise so the hook (or ball) snags the clog.

3. Back the snake off slightly, then steadily push it in again while turning the handle clockwise until the object is solidly hooked.

4. Pull the object out of the drain.

5. Run water full force for a minute or two to make sure the drain is fully unclogged.

6. If the blockage is stubborn (like tree roots), you may need to rent a commercial "power" auger with a rotor or blade that chops up whatever is in the line. This bigger project would be a great moment to HAP.

SAFETY Wear rubber gloves and safety glasses. (You never know what's going to squirt back toward you out of the sink!)

Tub Drains

If the pop-up in your bathtub drain doesn't open or sit properly, your tub may drain slowly or, worse, drain when you don't want it to. Adjusting it is easy.

TUFF CHIX DICTIONARY

A bathtub pop-up is a two-part mechanism: first, there's the stopper, which has a rocker arm that extends back toward the drain, and second, there's the overflow assembly, a lever that lifts or lowers a rod with a springlike end. When you flip the overflow lever up, it pushes the rod down onto the stopper's rocker arm, which raises the stopper. Flip the lever up, and it lifts the rod, allowing the stopper to drop down and plug the drain. Depending upon the type of pop-up, you adjust the way the stopper sits either by adjusting the length of the striker rod or by adjusting the rocker arm.

TUFF METER: 6

TIMER: 30 minutes

TUFF TOOLS: Screwdriver

SHOPPING LIST: Nothing

TOTAL PRICE: $0

$95–$125

1

2

2

How to adjust the overflow assembly:

1. Remove the screws that secure the overflow cover plate, and pull the plate and lever away from the overflow hole, partially pulling out the mechanism.

2. Adjust the nut that lengthens or shortens the rod assembly—lengthen it to raise the stopper higher, or shorten it to let it drop lower.

3. Push the assembly back in and screw the cover plate back into place.

How to adjust the stopper:

1. Lift the stopper out of the drain.

2. Clean off any hair or debris, and adjust the nut on the stopper's underside to shorten or lengthen its connection to the rocker arm.

3. Work the arm and stopper back down into the drain hole.

Faucet (Tap) Repair

Leaking water faucets won't just drive you crazy—they are also costly. Small leaks can waste gallons of water each day, and besides the environmental waste, seemingly small drips can create permanent water spots and stains in the base of your sink.

When you learn that most faucets with washers can be fixed in about half an hour—and for less than a dollar—you'll wonder why you didn't learn to do this years ago! If the constant drip in your sink is driving you crazy, learn to fix the faucet yourself (and save yourself time and money).

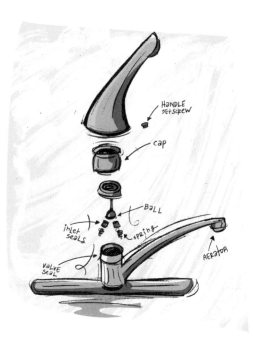

CAUSES OF LEAKS

Loose nuts If water is leaking around the base of the handle, your connection is probably just loose. Use an adjustable wrench and tighten the nut located just below the handle. (Note: In some faucets, the nut may be located inside a designer handle. If so, simply pull the handle off to reveal the faucet's hardware.)

Washer trouble The majority of faucet leaks are caused by washers that are worn, poorly installed, or the wrong size. Signs of poor washers include water that drips or runs out of the handles, slow leaks coming from the faucet, and water that collects or pools around the back of the faucet's handles.

TUFF CHIX DICTIONARY

There are many types of faucets on the market today. Even though they may look different, they all have the same basic parts and are put together in the same basic fashion. Most baths and bathrooms have "mixing faucets" or "stem faucets," which allow the user to select temperature settings by controlling the hot and cold handles. Mixing faucets and stem faucets have two separate units, either or both of which may need to be repaired.

If you're working with a stem faucet, you can determine which unit is leaking by shutting off the water supply in stages. Begin by turning off the hot water. If the leak has stopped dripping, it is the hot water valve unit's washer you'll need to replace. If not, try the cold. Follow the steps below to replace old washers with new ones.

FIXING A FAULTY WASHER

TUFF METER: 5

TIMER: 45 minutes

TUFF TOOLS: **Adjustable wrench, screwdriver**

SHOPPING LIST: **Washers of various sizes**

TOTAL PRICE: **Varies** $95–$145

How to fix a faulty washer:

1. Locate the valve and turn off the main water supply to the sink you're working on. This is *the* most important step, otherwise you'll be knee-deep in water with your first turn of the wrench! You'll find the shutoff valve close to the faucet you're repairing. It's usually located under the sink basin or inside a floor cabinet. Double-check that you've turned the water source off by turning on the faucet (hot and cold, if you're working with a mixed faucet). If no water comes out, you're ready for step two.

2. *Always* close the drain before attempting any faucet repair. This will prevent parts from slipping down into the drain as you're working. Oops—and it's gone!

3. Most faucet handles are secured by a screw, which is often covered by a snap-on cap. You'll need to pry this off either with your hands or gently with a flat-head screwdriver, and remove the screw before loosening the packing nut.

4. Turning counterclockwise, loosen the packing nut. (The packing nut is located just below or inside the individual faucet handles. If you have designer faucet handles, you first need to remove the decorative covering.) Using the faucet handle, pull out the entire valve unit by twisting and turning it until it pulls free.

5. Holding the valve unit in your hand, locate the old washer. (It will most likely be at the bottom of the valve unit itself.) Remove the screw that is holding the old washer in place.

6. Using the old washer as your size guide, replace it with one of equal size. It should fit snugly into the circular lip without forced pressure. Now replace the screw.

7. Run your finger inside the area where the stem assembly enters the faucet to find out whether the stem seat is rough or grooved. If so, it will need replacing with a new valve seat that exactly matches the old one in diameter, height, and threads.

8. Place the valve unit back into the faucet, turning the handle to its proper position before tightening.

9. Tighten the packing nut and turn the water back on. Test for leaks.

10. If your faucet continues to leak and you're fairly certain the washer is to blame, try replacing the old washer with one of a different size.

FAUCET PROBLEMS AND SOLUTIONS

PROBLEM	REASON	SOLUTION
Dripping: Faucet drips from the end of the spout.	There are loose parts within the faucet. Can be fixed if it is the parts. If it's the faucet itself, must replace the faucet.	• Tighten any loose parts by hand or by a wrench. • If it still leaks, start to take the faucet apart and replace any worn washers. • If spout continues to leak, replace the entire faucet.
Leaks: Faucet leaks from the base.	There are loose parts within the faucet. Can be fixed if it is the parts. If it's the faucet itself, must replace the faucet.	• Take the faucet apart and tighten (or replace) any loose connections or washers or O-rings. • If faucet continues to leak, replace the entire faucet.
Leaks: Faucet leaks onto floor from underneath the faucet.	There could be a variety of reasons. You could have bad hoses or bad connections. Either way, get this fixed *immediately*, as water in the cupboard or floor can lead to mold or rot.	• Find the source: Is it the base of the faucet? The hoses? The shut-off valves? Check both the hot and cold water lines. Determine where the leak is coming from. • Base of faucet: Tighten any connections. • Hoses: If the supply hoses are cracked or damaged, replace hose(s). If the connection between the hose and the valves is loose, tighten them. • Shutoff valves: Tighten connection at both the hose and the wall connection. If still leaking, replace the shutoff valve(s).
Water sputters from spout.	This is most likely due to air in your lines.	• Let water run from each line. This should fix the problem. • If it doesn't, you will need to locate the source of the air leaking into the line. Check all the connections, the hoses, and the pipes. If there is air getting in, there will most likely be water leaking out.

FAUCET PROBLEMS AND SOLUTIONS

PROBLEM	REASON	SOLUTION
Low water pressure (or water sprays crazily from spout).	The easy reason: The tiny screen located inside the faucet is blocked, therefore restricting water flow. The not-so-easy reason: This could be because there is low pressure in the lines. The water is either being restricted through a "pressure-reducing valve" or your pipes are corroded. This is more commonly found in old galvanized pipes.	• Unscrew end of faucet. Clean out tiny little screen (usually little rocks) and replace. • Still low pressure? It's your lines. You can do one of two things: 1. Check your pipes. If they are corroded, you may be losing pressure because water is simply leaking out or air is getting in creating a loose passageway. Replace corroded galvanized pipes and with copper—HAP for that one. 2. Check to see if your line has a "pressure-reducing valve" (usually located outside near the house). Release a bit at a time to allow more flow and therefore add pressure.
Showerhead leaks (or sprays crazily from head).	This is usually due to dirt or debris in your showerhead.	• With the water off, unscrew the sprayer head and clean thoroughly. • Clean the connections with a cloth or a wire brush for any buildup. • Replace showerhead and screw on tight to avoid leaks from the base.

Tuff Tips

- Lubricate all parts of the stem assembly with plumber's (heat-proof) grease to improve the seal.
- By wrapping the jaws of your pliers or wrench with masking or duct tape you'll prevent marring and damaging the soft metal parts of your faucet.

- Pay attention to the order in which you're removing parts so that you know how to re-assemble them when you're finished.
- It's not a bad idea to replace washers for both the hot and cold water, even if only one is leaking. It's worth noting, however, that washers for handles controlling hot water wear out twice as fast as those that control cold water.

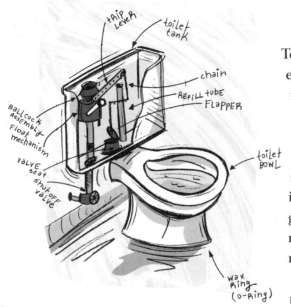

Toilets

Toilets may look (and sometimes even smell) scary, but really they're made up of quite simple parts. And though some of the names of the parts will be foreign to you, they're actually put together in a pretty simple way. So if your toilet is leaking, running, or rocking, there's no good reason to put off fixing it, and most of the time there's no good reason to call in a professional.

As with all other plumbing jobs, make your very first task to shut off the water supply to the toilet by closing the valve, which is almost always located right underneath the toilet.

REPLACING A TOILET SEAT

Let's start with the easy things first—replacing your toilet seat. If your toilet seat is in bad shape, won't stay on the toilet, or just needs updating, this is a quick and easy way to give your toilet a fresh, new look. The last thing you want is for your seat to move around when, well, you are taking care of business.

As a matter of fact, I just performed this little operation this week. We were staying at a fancy hotel and my travel companion (Mercury,

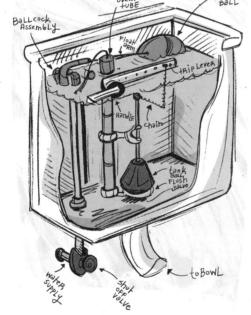

Tuff Tip

Whenever you are investigating the inner workings of your toilet, be sure to carefully remove the tank lid and set it aside. Since it is made out of porcelain, it tends to chip more easily than you might think.

my kitty) noticed that the toilet had a fancy seat—one of those concave, rounded types. Oh, I guess this is a good time to tell you that Mercury uses the toilet, not a litter box. Really, you might ask? Yes, really. It's not as difficult as you might think to train them to use such facilities. I can tell you all about the twelve-step process involved, but for now, let's get back to the subject. Mercury can't manage those fancy seats so I went to the hardware store and bought the cheapest toilet seat they had and put that on the toilet. Mercury was happy, thus making me happy. The point to this little diversion is that doing this is easy and can be performed anywhere.

TUFF METER: **2**

TIMER: 20 minutes

TUFF TOOLS: Screwdriver, pliers

SHOPPING LIST: Toilet seat ($14.99–$39.99)

TOTAL PRICE: $14.99

$125

How to replace a toilet seat:

Out with the old:

1. Remove your old toilet seat, which is held in place with two bolts located at the back of the seat.

2. In order to access these bolts, you may need to lift the small plastic covers.

3. With your screwdriver, steady the bolts from the top and reach your hand below the seat to unscrew the nuts. You may need pliers for this if the nuts stick. You can also hold the nut underneath and unscrew the bolt with your screwdriver from the top.

4. Remove seat and set it aside—in the trash can.

5. Be sure to clean around the holes—scrub if you must—to remove any dirt or rust.

In with the new:

1. Typically, toilet seats come in two standard sizes: a regular (round) or elongated bowl. Check to see which type you have before buying and attempting to install a new one.

2. Place the new seat over the toilet, making sure that it fits over the mounting holes.

3. Put the new bolts in and tighten the nuts underneath with your hands.

4. When the nuts are hand tight, grab them with your pliers. With your other hand, tighten the bolts with your screwdriver. Be careful! These bolts are usually plastic and will break if you overtighten them. If the screws are made of a tougher material, then you could crack the porcelain if you attempt to overtighten them. So be careful.

5. If the new toilet seat comes with bolt covers, snap them into place.

FIXING CLOGS

There are two main kinds of plungers: suction-cup plungers and force-ball plungers. Suction-cup plungers are more common, but if it doesn't do the job, you can usually open a clogged toilet by using a force-ball plunger. A force-ball plunger exerts a great deal more pressure than the regular type for clearing toilets.

FORCE BALL PLUNGER

TUFF METER: 4

TIMER: 10 minutes (depending on how deep the clog is)

TUFF TOOLS: Plunger, closet auger (or snake), adjustable wrench, screwdriver, plumber's greas

SHOPPING LIST: Washers of various sizes

TOTAL PRICE: Varies $75–$125

Everyone has a plunger in the house, but do you really know how to use one? Many people think you move the plunger up and down in the toilet until the blockage is cleared. Actually, it's quite the contrary. You should be able to clear a clog with one pass. Here's how:

1. Take your plunger and put it directly over the toilet drain. Set it down gently, making sure you have a good seal between the plunger and the drain.

2. With one hefty downward motion, push the plunger down. Providing you had a good seal, this will push

Tuff Tip

To test if you have successfully removed the blockage, *don't* flush with the handle. Instead, to see whether water is moving through easily, remove the tank lid and let out small amounts of water by manually opening and closing the flapper (or drop ball).

down the water you had trapped between the plunger and drain. The force of this motion should send the clog on its way.

3. Repeat if necessary.

How to fix toilet clogs:

1. Make sure there's enough water in the toilet bowl when using the plunger. It should have as much as is normally there. If it doesn't, add a bit of water with a cup or bucket.

2. If the plunger does not clear the clogged drain, use a closet snake, or auger (see, p. 175). Start the snake into the bowl and continue to crank it until it becomes tight. This cranking and pulling action will usually bring up the object that is causing the stoppage.

3. If you're still having no luck, you may need to remove the toilet from the floor, turn it upside down, and force the obstruction out from the top or bottom.

4. If you must remove the toilet from the floor, use a wax preformed O-ring to reseat the toilet (see below, p. 188).

REPAIRING RUNNING TOILETS

A running toilet can be simple thing to fix, and the water savings will add up quickly.

Repairing a running toilet will require you to figure out where the problem is coming from. Follow the instructions below to locate your source. Some of these mechanisms you may want to test when the tank is full. Others, when the tank is empty. Feel it out. If you need to empty the tank, turn the water off at the shutoff valve and flush the toilet.

How to repair a running toilet:

1. Check the guide rod and chain on the tank stopper. If the rod is bent or the chain links are twisted just straighten them.

2. Check the float mechanism. If lifting the ball up stops the water from running, try to bend the float arm *up* slightly to get the right buoyancy.

3. Conversely, if water spills into the overflow tube, bend the float arm *down*. If the ball has water in it, it needs to be replaced. Remove it by unscrewing it from the arm.

4. If the toilet is still running, the valve seat and stopper may have corrosion or buildup preventing the stopper from closing. Lift the stopper up and check for any buildup or damage or objects that might be preventing it from sitting correctly. Gently scour the area. If there is a great deal of damage replace the stopper and valve seat.

5. The flush valve assembly may have to be replaced if the toilet is still running. Take the old parts with you when

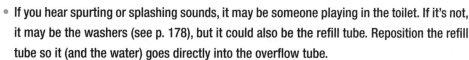

Tuff Tips

- If your toilet is making a whistling sound, replace the washers in the ballcock-valve plunger. Remember to use plumber's grease to help seal and preserve your new washers.
- If you hear spurting or splashing sounds, it may be someone playing in the toilet. If it's not, it may be the washers (see p. 178), but it could also be the refill tube. Reposition the refill tube so it (and the water) goes directly into the overflow tube.
- If your toilet is only partially flushing, try bending the float arm upward to raise the water level (as in step 2, above) or shortening the lift chain.

purchasing the new gaskets and assembly to ensure a perfect match. If the shaft of the assembly is cracked, the whole shaft and assembly will need to be replaced. Again, take the flush valve assembly with you to get a perfect match.

REPAIRING LEAKY TOILETS

The sound of a trickling stream or fountain can be romantic, but not if it's your toilet running continuously. The problem could be a leaky tank seal. Before you buy replacement parts, open the tank and raise the ball or flapper away from the overflow valve. Then scour the valve seat with fine steel wool or a plastic scouring pad. Sometimes mineral deposits can collect there, making it hard to form a watertight seal, and causing your toilet to run.

REMOVING OR REPLACING THE WAX RING

Toilets are fixed to the drainpipe with a ring of wax, which acts as a sealant and keeps smells where they should be—in the pipes! A wax seal will lose its grip if the toilet moves even a little bit, and that's your first red flag. Don't put this off, because it's not hard and it will save you from damage or mold that could accumulate under the toilet. So change your wax ring!

You'll also know it's time to change the wax ring when:

- Water leaks from the base of the toilet
- The toilet rocks back and forth—even just a little bit (after you have tightened the bolts)
- The bathroom smells bad long *after* it should; that is, you can smell sewage constantly
- The toilet is moved for flooring replacement or repair

If your toilet leaks at the base, first try tightening the bolts at the base of the bowl before changing to the wax

TUFF METER: **6**   (because of the weight of the toilet)

TIMER: 45 minutes

TUFF TOOLS: Adjustable wrench, scraper

SHOPPING LIST: Wax (or O-) ring ($1.42–$5.99)

TOTAL PRICE: $1.42   **$110–$210**

ring. If you do change the ring, don't forget to shut off the valve!

How to change the wax ring on your toilet (or how to set your toilet back in place):

1. Turn off the water supply at the base of the toilet. In order to get rid of all the excess water still in the toilet, flush after the water is shut off. This should drain the tank.

2. Loosen and remove the nuts and bolts at the base of the toilet. All but the oldest toilet bolts will be covered with some kind of decorative/concealing cap. Usually these can be removed with a simple prying action.

3. Get a friend to help you tip the toilet over or lift it away. Have towels standing by for any additional water that is left in the toilet. Set the toilet aside.

4. Scrape off the old wax ring. The old wax ring will look *nothing* like the new one, so don't be alarmed. It squishes down and turns brown after being under a toilet. Make sure you scrape away all the old wax.

TOILET PROBLEMS AND SOLUTIONS

PROBLEMS	REASONS	SOLUTIONS
Toliet will not flush.	The chain could be loose or have fallen off, or the water could be turned off at the shutoff valve.	• Make sure water is turned on at the shut-off valve. • Check the lift chain or lift wires. Tighten or reconnect as necessary.
Toilet overflows when flushed, or flushes slowly.	There is a clog in your toilet or the main pipe.	• First use a plunger to clear the clog. • If there is visible debris, remove debris with a rubber glove. • If this does not clear the clog, remove the toilet and clear the main pipe with a snake.
Toilet runs or drips continuously.	The inner makings of the toilet are loose, have fallen off, or are in need of replacing.	• Adjust lift wires or lift chain. • Replace leaky float ball. • Adjust water level in tank. • Adjust and clean flush valve. • Repair or replace ball cock.
Toilet handle is tough to push and/ or sticks.	Could be debris around handle, wires, or chain. Lift wires could be too tight.	• Adjust lift wires. • Clean and adjust handle. It may be as simple as removing any rust buildup.
Toilet handle is loose or droopy.	Handle has fallen off or drooped from lift chain and/or wires.	• Adjust handle. • Reattach lift chain or lift wires to lever.
Water on floor around toilet.	The toilet is leaking at a connection point. This could be due to loose bolts, wax ring, or a crack in the porcelain.	• Tighten tank bolts and water connection. • Insulate tank to prevent condensation. • Replace wax ring. • Replace cracked tank or bowl.

5. Lay the new ring down in its place.

6. Carefully lift the toilet, with your partner, and put it back in place. Make sure the bolts from the floor are aligned with the holes in the toilet base. Push down on the toilet so that it makes a good seal with the wax ring.

7. Screw the nuts to the bolts and cover with their caps.

6

Garbage Disposals

I'm not going to tell you how to replace a broken garbage disposal in this book—you'll have to advance to my next book for that! But if the blades of your dispoal are blunt, try one of these two tricks: ice or glass.

Throwing a bunch of ice down your disposal while it's running will sharpen the blades. So will broken glass. I don't recommend breaking a glass just for the job, but when you do accidentally break one, turn on the water and wash a little bit of the glass down the drain with the disposal running. Rule: *Always* have the water running when your disposal is switched on.

Tubb Tip

If your disposal drain smells, try chopping up a lemon—take the seeds out first—and whizzing half of it down the drain. It will give it a fresh lemon smell, and the natural acid in the lemon should also help kill the germs that are the source of the problem.

Washing-Machine Hoses

This is easy, easy, easy! If you've ever attached a garden hose to an outdoor tap or spray nozel, doing this is exactly the same level of difficulty. And spending between ten and twenty dollars could save you thousands of dollars in potentially damaged floor coverings, furniture, and other valuables in your home that might be ruined by an uninvited deluge.

Washing-machine hoses come in varying thicknesses and can be found at most hardware stores. Some hoses on the market have preformed metal attachments designed to prevent them from kinking. As with all your projects, *ask* someone at the store if you're not sure what is best for your machine, and take the worn hoses with you as examples.

It pays to inspect your washing-machine hoses regularly and to take preventative maintenance steps. Most hoses need replacing about every three to five years, but it might be a good idea to change them every year, just to be sure. If you notice any cracks or signs of wear and tear, follow these easy steps.

TUFF METER: 3

 TIMER: 20 minutes

TUFF TOOLS: Adjustable wrench

 SHOPPING LIST: Washing-machine hoses

 TOTAL PRICE: $7 each $65–$125, plus materials

How to replace washing-machine hoses:

1. Shut off the water supply to your washing machine. There should be shutoff valves for each hose: the hot water and the cold water. If there is no accessible valve directly near the washer, shut off the entire water supply to your house. *This is very important!*

2. Detach the old hoses and hook the new ones up. You can usually do this by hand, but you may need an adjustable wrench to get started. Make sure you line up the threads perfectly and screw the hoses on tightly by hand. Use the wrench to make sure they are tight.

3. Turn the water supply back on, opening it just a little at a time and checking for leaks.

Tuff Tips

- Check your replaced hoses to make sure they are free of kinks or bends that are at too tight an angle.
- Leave at least four inches between the water connection and the back of the machine. This will reduce the chances of kinks.

Types of Pipes

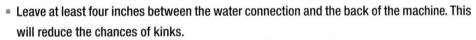

What are those pipes around your house? Here's a chart to show you what your pipes are, and what you would need to repair them if needed.

TYPE OF PIPE	DESCRIPTION	TOOLS FOR CUTTING & REPLACING
Cast iron *(Gray pipe)*	These pipes are used for draining. More popular in the past, they are still used today, but PVC is typically now used for the same application. These are commonly found under your house or building.	Cast iron pipes are very strong, which makes them difficult to cut and replace. Cut with a hacksaw or cast iron cutter. Join with hubbed fittings.
PVC (Polyvinyl chloride) *(White plastic pipe)*	These pipes are used for draining, venting, and traps. They are also used for irrigation and sprinkler systems. They are currently the best and most widely used material for these installations PVC is a stiff, thick, unbendable plastic that is very durable and difficult to damage by heat or chemicals. It can handle a lot of pressure, but can crack if frozen.	PVC pipes are easy to cut, join and replace. Cut with a hacksaw or PVC cutter. Join with solvent glue and PVC joints and fittings.These are so easy to work with that I often use them for other applications while I'm theming a room.
ABS (Acrylonitrile butadiene styrene) *(Black plastic pipe)*	These pipes are used for draining, venting, and traps. This type of pipe is also stiff plastic, and was the first of the plastic pipes to be used in homes. They are typically not used for new application	Follow PVC instructions. They are a little tougher to work with, but not much.
Chrome *(Shiny silver pipe)*	These pipes are typically used in places where you can see them, therefore you want it to look good (bathroom traps, valves, shutoffs, etc.).	Chrome pipes will be harder to cut. Use a hacksaw or reciprocating saw. Join with compression fittings or solder.

TYPE OF PIPE	DESCRIPTION	TOOLS FOR CUTTING & REPLACING
Galvanized iron *(Matte gray pipe)*	These pipes are *very* strong but will corrode away in time. They are usually in older homes/buildings and are not used for new installations. They are used for hot and cold water supply lines and drains.	These are very difficult to cut, so I would suggest HAP. If you attempt to tackle it, use a reciprocating saw or hacksaw. Join with galvanized threaded fittings.
Black Iron *(Dark gray/black pipe)*	These pipes look a lot like galvanized iron but black iron pipes are smaller in diameter and are used for gas, not plumbing.	These are also difficult to cut, and since they deal with gas, I would *strongly* suggest HAP. Use a reciprocating saw or hacksaw to cut and join with black iron threaded fittings.
PE or poly (Polyethylene) *(Black or dark blue pipe)*	This pipe is black or dark blue. It is used for irrigation systems (sprinklers) and sometimes for main water supply. Typically only used for cold water applications, because it stands up to freezing temperatures. It is not the best, though, for handling a lot of pressure.	PE pipes are easy to cut, similar to PVC. Use plastic pipe cutter, hacksaw, reciprocating saw, or miter saw. To join, use PVC fittings and/or stainless steel hose clamps.
Copper *(Shiny orange copper)*	Copper pipes are usually smaller in diameter, used for gas pipes.	Copper is fairly easy to cut, provided you have the right tool. Get a copper pipe cutter. Join with metal brass fittings and/or compression fittings, in conjunction with solder.

Tuff Tip

Be sure that you get the correct solvent or glue for your pipes. Each pipe requires a different application.

ELECTRICAL REPAIRS

This remains one of my *very* favorite subjects: electricity! Why? Because it seems so scary, but it's really so easy and can make such a big difference in your home.

I work with a makeup artist, Tracey, who uses electricity (lighting, in particular) to her advantage on a daily basis. When you walk into her home, you just feel beautiful. Why? Because she has picked the right colors for the walls and *lighting* that is very flattering. Even in her bathroom, the light cast upon you in the mirror makes you feel beautiful. What's her secret? Well, she told me that people give her compliments when she wears yellow. Thus, she has chosen yellow tones for her home—from the lighting to wall colors—and as a result feels beautiful. Is there a color you wear that makes people compliment you? You might want to think about incorporating that color into your home.

Lighting can be such an important part of a home. Outdoors and indoors, it can make your home more beautiful, and even more safe. When you pull up to a home that is perfectly lit, with small lights cast up trees, against the house, and lighting the pathway to the front door, it makes whatever work you have done to your house come to life. Or, when harsh floodlights come on when motion sensors are activated, it can provide an inexpensive way to increase the safety and security of your home. The same is true inside the house. Whether you want to light your favorite painting, light the kitchen for cooking, light the bedroom for a different kind of cooking, or set up a timer to fend off burglars, the correct lighting is essential.

Choosing a Light

Lighting is a whole universe unto itself, with dozens of options—from fluorescent to halogen. When buying lights, it pays to do a little research. Search around on the Internet, and as with almost all jobs, talk to a salesperson about your individual needs and what the local codes are for interior lighting. I know that in California, for instance, bathrooms and kitchens must have fluorescent lighting (not the most flattering, ladies). Check with your local building department for codes and requirements.

But lighting is just the beginning.

Safety: Don't Be Afraid!

Don't be scared by the thought of working with electricity—but *do* be extra cautious. Remember to ALWAYS turn off the power at the main switch in the fuse box before beginning any work of an electrical nature.

When you test your work, don't be afraid. If you have wired it wrong, it will simply "trip the breaker," meaning, it will turn off the switch at your fuse box. It will not blow up the house. If the breaker is tripped, it simply means that you have wired something wrong. Don't panic—just go back and repeat the steps until it works correctly.

A word of advice: do NOT work when you are tired. I have found that when I'm tired, electricity and I are *not* friends.

Finding the Main Power Supply

The circuit breaker or fuse box will be a metal or plastic box, about the size of a shoebox (or bigger, depending on the size of your apartment or house) attached to the wall. The fuse

> **SAFETY:** At the risk of being repetitive, this will be step one in every project dealing with electricity. Anytime you're doing electrical work, make sure that the power to the circuit you're working on is turned OFF at the main breaker box or fuse panel. For extra precaution, stick a large note on the breaker or fuse box saying that you are working and that the power supply should remain off—just in case someone else comes along and decides to be "helpful" and turn it back on for you.
>
> *(cont.)*

box regulates the flow of electricity into different parts of the house.

The most likely place for the fuse box will be the garage or the basement. If you are in an apartment building, the box can be anywhere—from inside a cupboard to hanging on an outside wall in some obscure passageway. The best idea is to ask your neighbor or property manager.

Older houses usually have fuse boxes instead of circuit breakers. Circuit breakers and fuses guard against fires and electrocution by tripping the breakers or blowing the fuses to cut off the power supply if the wires are in danger of over-heating. Open the box and look inside for the fuses or circuit breakers (see page 22 in the introduction).

(see page 22 in the introduction)

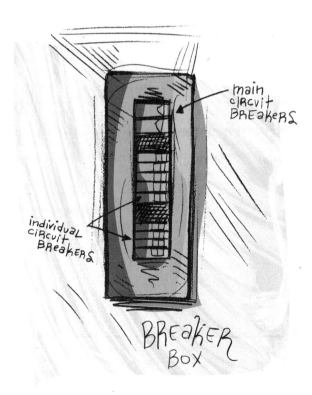

main circuit BReakers

individual ciRcuit BReakers

BReakeR Box

Changing Light Switches

Changing the light switches throughout your home or apartment can give the place a new feel. In rental properties, I often change all the dingy yellow light switches and receptacles to bright white ones. It is an inexpensive way to make the whole place seem a little cleaner and newer.

While you are at it, you can change the switch plate covers to the same color, too. These are usually plastic, but they come in a variety of different materials, shapes, and sizes. If you find that a cover is not covering the hole properly, you can buy a larger one. Most home improvement stores sell both a standard size and a larger size.

TUFF METER: 4

 TIMER: 30 minutes

TUFF TOOLS: Wire stripper, screwdrivers (Phillips and tiny flat-head) or a cordless drill and screwdriver attachment, circuit tester

 SHOPPING LIST: Replacement light switch(es) ($0.49–$25)

TOTAL PRICE: $0.49   **$75 (most electricians will charge a 2-hour minimum)**

How to change a light switch:

1. Turn off the power at the main circuit breaker or fuse box.

2. Test to be sure that the power is off by flipping the light switch on the wall.

3. With a screwdriver, remove the two screws holding the cover plate. (The piece of metal or plastic covering the switch.)

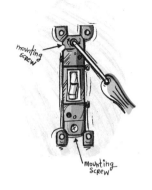

4. Take the cover plate off. You'll now see the electrical box. For extra safety, you can now test the circuit with a circuit tester to make doubly sure that it is not receiving any power.

5. Remove the two mounting screws holding the switch in place inside the electrical box.

6. Pull the switch out of the wall. The switch should come out a few inches, exposing the wires, which are usually color coded. You should see three separate wires: the black wire, also called the "hot" wire; the white wire, which is neutral: and a ground wire, which may be green or green/yellow and is sometimes a bare copper wire attached to a green screw. Depending on when your home was built, the ground wire may not be there at all.

7. Wires are attached to a switch in one of two ways: by being plugged in, or held on by another set of screws. Either unscrew and disconnect all the old wires from the old switch, or use a small flat-head screwdriver to release the wires from the old switch. It will fit in just above the wire hole-opening. Be sure to take note of which wire came from which screw. You can do this with colored crayons or pens, or with colored tape. (Sometimes the wires and screws will already be coded.)

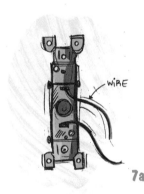

8. If the wires are in good condition—that is, not frayed, and neatly exposed from the rubber insulation—you will be able to skip to the next step. Otherwise, you'll

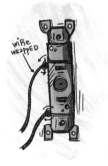

need to cut each wire the *minimum* amount, back to the rubber casing. Next, with a wire stripper, remove a bit of the rubber from the end of each wire.

8

9. Take the switch to the hardware store and get another one exactly like it. Ask a salesperson for help if necessary.

10. Hold the new switch up to the wall, taking note of the position of the words *off* and *on,* to make sure that you don't screw in the switch upside down. (Seems obvious, but I must say it: *off* is down.)

11. Take the switch away from the wall and attach the wires to the screws on its back or sides according to the color-coded tags. Insert each wire—with the proper amount of wire exposed on both the black and white— into the switch terminal on the back of the new switch. If you find that a wire does not fit and won't go into the back of the receptacle, you will need to bend the wire around the screw on the side of the receptacle. Tighten the wires to the unit with a screwdriver.

12. Don't forget about the ground wire. This is usually the copper-colored wire that attaches to a green screw on the switch. Although this does not supply power, it will ground the switch to reduce electrical shock. Wrap it around the green screw and tighten the screw to affix the wire to the switch.

13. With all three wires connected, the switch is ready to install in the wall box.

14. Secure the new switch in the box with mounting screws, making sure it is right side up.

15. Replace the switch cover.

16. Turn the main power back on and flip the switch to see if you've passed the test!

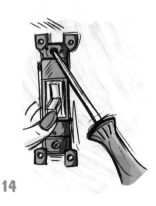

14

Tuff Tip

Marking which wire was attached to which screw will prevent wiring mix-ups. This can be especially important if are unknowingly working with a three-way switch: that is, a single light controlled from two locations. You can mark the wires by wrapping a small piece of tape around them—just make sure you remove it before finishing the project. You can also used colored pens or crayons.

TROUBLESHOOTING: LIGHT FIXTURE PROBLEMS AND SOLUTIONS

PROBLEM	REASON	SOLUTION
Light fixture mounted on the wall or ceiling flickers or does not work.	Bulb could be burned out. Wires could be loose. Switch could be bad.	• Check the lightbulb. Replace if it's burned out. • Remove the plate cover and check the wall switch. Check all the wires for loose connections. • Replace wall switch, if needed. • If all else fails, replace light fixture.
Light fixture recessed in ceiling flickers or does not work.	Bulb could be burned out. Wires could be loose. Switch could be bad. Light fixture could be bad.	• Check the lightbulb. Replace if it's burned out. • Remove the plate cover and check the wall switch. Check all the wires for loose connections. • Replace wall switch, if needed. • If all else fails, replace light fixture.
Chandelier flickers or does not work.	Bulb could be burned out, or bulbs could be loose. Wires in the switch or chandelier could be loose. Switch could be bad. Chandelier could be bad.	• Check each individual lightbulb. Replace if it's burned out. • Remove the plate cover and check the wall switch. Check all the wires for loose connections. • Replace wall switch, if needed. • Check for loose wires on the fixture. • Check each individual light socket. Replace, if needed. • If all else fails, replace chandelier.

(cont.)

PROBLEM	REASON	SOLUTION
The switch on the light fixture does not work.	Bulb could be burned out. Wires could be loose. Switch could be bad. Light fixture could be bad.	• Check the light bulb. Replace if it's burned out. • Check for loose wire connections on built-in switch. • Replace switch if accessible. • If all else fails, replace light fixture.

Tuff Tip

If you have a remote control for the light or ceiling fan, check the batteries in the remote before troubleshooting the light.

Installing a Dimmer Switch

Mood, mood, mood! Installing one or more dimmer switches can change the entire feel of your rooms, making them warm, cozy—and, of course, romantic.

It's such a simple concept: Bright light in the bathroom when you're putting on makeup for a big night out. And then, with a simple touch of the fingers, low light in the same place when you want to take a relaxing bath. Bright light in the bedroom when you want to look for that pair of shoes in the back of the closet: low light when you want to, um—hide the dust from visitors!

Dimmer switches are very simple to install and can be picked up for as little as ten dollars in a hardware or lighting store.

Money, money, money! Dimmer switches aren't just about mood (and visitors). They will also increase the resale value of your home.

Dimmers come in a variety of models, ranging from dial switches to "up–down" dimmers to touch-sensitive dimmers. The latter are a little fancier—and more expensive—but I actually prefer the old-fashioned turn nobs.

TUFF METER: 4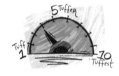

 TIMER: 30 minutes

TUFF TOOLS: Wire stripper, screwdrivers (Phillips and tiny flat-head)

 SHOPPING LIST: Dimmer switch(es) ($4.09–$67.95)

 TOTAL PRICE: $4.09 $95, plus materials

How to install a dimmer switch:

Installing a dimmer switch is the *exact* same procedure as installing a regular switch! It is that easy—but now instead of an on/off switch, you have mood at your fingertips.

So, follow the procedure above, with one change: In step 10, instead of "off" and "on," make sure that you install the switch so that "left" is dimmer and "right" is brighter. The same goes for a vertical dimmer: make sure that "up" is on/brighter and "down" is off/dimmer.

RECEPTACLE PROBLEMS AND REPAIRS

PROBLEM	REASON FOR PROBLEM	HOW TO FIX THE PROBLEM
Your appliance does not work when plugged into the receptacle.	You first want to access the source of the problem— make sure the appliance works by testing it in other receptacles, replacing bulb, checking cord, etc. If it still does not work, you have loose wires, dirty wires, or a faulty receptacle.	• Turn electricity off and tighten any loose wires, and/or connections. • Clean around all of the wires, even the ends. • If all else fails, replace the receptacle.
Your appliance plug keeps falling out of receptacle or stays loose.	You first want to make sure it's the receptacle and not the appliance plug. Try it in other receptacles. If it is still loose, your receptacle is worn and tired. There is no way to repair it— it must be replaced.	• Replace the receptacle.
Your receptacle sparks or buzzes when you plug something in or take it out, or it warms up and is even hot to the touch.	Your receptacle is most likely wired incorrectly or wires are loose, but it could also be an accumulation of dust or dirt, an overload, or simply a faulty receptacle.	• You can try to move appliances to other receptacles to assure you are not overloading it. If you still have trouble: • Turn electricity off and tighten any loose wires and/or connections. • Clean around all of the wires, even the ends. • If all else fails, replace the receptacle.

RECEPTACLE PROBLEMS AND REPAIRS

PROBLEM	REASON FOR PROBLEM	HOW TO FIX THE PROBLEM
Fuse box alert! Your circuit breaker keeps tripping and turning electricity off, or your fuse keeps burning out right after you replace it.	This could be the fault of the appliance—could be an overload or faulty cords. Check wattage & cord condition. Could also be that the receptacle has loose wires or experiencing a build up of dust and dirt.	• You can try to move appliances to other receptacles to assure you are not overloading it. Also fix any faulty or damaged cords. If you still have trouble: • Turn electricity off and tighten any loose wires and/or connections • Clean around all of the wires, even the ends. • If all else fails, replace the receptacle.

Replacing an Electrical Receptacle

Like changing light switches, changing electrical receptacles (outlets) can give your place a new feel. Function might also play a part as well. Do you notice that your receptacles are not holding on to the plugs for your appliances? If they are loose, it can be very frustrating (especially when it comes to vacuuming or curling your hair).

Like with light switches, you can change the receptacle plate covers to a new, clean color. You will be surprised what a difference this small touch can make in your home.

TUFF METER: 4

TIMER: 30 minutes

TUFF TOOLS: Wire stripper, screwdrivers (Phillips and flat-head)

SHOPPING LIST: Electrical receptacles ($0.99–$5)

TOTAL PRICE: $0.99 $75, plus materials

How to replace an electrical receptacle:

Guess what? Installing an electrical receptacle is almost exactly like installing its sisters—the light switch and dimmer switch.

Here are a couple of changes: In step 10, you don't have to test for "right side up." At step 14, however, you do. Make sure when you install the receptacle that it *is* right side up—should it look like a little face.

Oh, and I probably don't have to tell you this, but I will. In step 16, instead of "flipping the switch," plug something into your new receptacle to see if it works.

Installing a Ceiling Fan

A ceiling fan is another one of my favorite features—and not just for its most obvious benefit of cooling your jets in the summer. A fan can increase the value of your property, at very little cost in terms of money or effort. Plus, it doesn't require any more power than a normal light switch, making the upgrade to a ceiling fan even more appealing. If the fan also has lights on it, however, make sure that it won't overload your circuit. Check on the manufacturer's instructions to see what it requires.

flush mount

Ceiling fans are easy to install if there is already a light fixture in place in the exact spot where you want the fan (usually right in the center of the room). This is the project I've outlined below. If there is no existing light fixture, the task becomes a lot trickier, and I recommend that you HAP.

There are "flush mount" fans that sit directly on the wall and "drop rod mount" fans, which are sent down away from the ceiling. There should always be at least seven feet of space between the bottom of your fan and the floor. If your ceilings are too low, do *not* attempt to put in a ceiling fan.

Drop Rod mount

So, how high should you go if you have the luxury of high ceilings? It's really up to you and what you think will look best. You can have a drop rod as long as two feet or as short as four inches.

How big of a fan should you choose? The bigger the room, the bigger the fan. Don't try to put a large (say fifty-two-inch) fan in a small room—it will overpower the room.

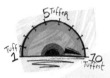

TUFF METER: 10

TIMER: 1 hour

TUFF TOOLS: Wire stripper, cordless drill with screwdriver attachment, screwdrivers, ladder

SHOPPING LIST: Ceiling fan kit ($90 and up)

TOTAL PRICE: $90 $385, plus materials (fan)

How to install a ceiling fan:

1. Turn off the power to the light at the circuit breaker or fuse.

2. Carefully read the fan manufacturer's instructions to see what product-specific installation tools you might need.

3. Carefully remove the old light. Make sure you have had the light turned off for a while so it is cool to the touch.

4. Disconnect the wires. You should see three separate wires: the black wire, also called the "hot" wire; the white wire, which is neutral; and a ground wire, which may be green or green/yellow and is sometimes a bare copper wire attached to a green screw. Depending on when your home was built, this ground wire may not be there at all. Do this by unscrewing the wire nuts. Wire nuts work just like nuts over a screw—they bind the wires together. Keep these wire nuts to use with the new wires. If the wires are merely taped together, unwrap the tape and use wire nuts for the new installation.

5. Look at the junction box (the enclosed and protected box where the wires and stuff are held). Is it plastic? If so, you will need to replace it with a metal box that will withstand more weight. If the box is metal, you are good to go.

6. Install the mounting brackets for the fan kit to the electrical box. Make sure that the screws and connections are *really* tight. You don't want a wobbly fan!

7. You will now need to assemble the fan. Follow the manufacturer's instructions for the unit you buy, since the assembly of every ceiling fan is different.

8. The instructions will always tell you to put the fan blades on *after* you have hung the unit, but I find that it is difficult to fasten and screw the blades to the unit when it's installed. Check to see

SAFETY: You need a ladder for this project, and anytime you do this kind of work you really should have someone standing by just in case you fall. Ditto for electrical work. Even though I know the first thing you are going to do is make sure that the main breaker box or fuse panel is switched off, it doesn't hurt to have a backup work partner around in the unlikely event that something should go wrong.

What should this helpful partner do if you become electrocuted? Haul off and hit you. Sounds harsh, I know, but they must hit you quickly and with enough force that it will knock the power source out of your hands. If they simply nudge you, they run the risk of electrocution as well, and you are both doomed. So do your friend a favor— hit 'em!

if there will be enough room to get your screwdriver between the ceiling and the blades. If not, put them on before. If so, you can go ahead and wait.

9. Have your helper hold the fan high enough so that you can attach the wires from the fan to the wires in the junction box. Attach the wires according to color (black to black, white to white, green to ground wire). Use wire nuts to cover each connection. Screw the nut on over the connection and twist until tight.

10. Push all excess wire up into the electrical box. Keep pushing until it is all tucked away.

11. Attach the fan motor to the mounting bracket. The appropriate screws should be in the kit.

12. While you still have it somewhat open, turn the power back on to make sure that all of your electrical work is good. You don't want to get completely done and find out that one of your connections is bad. Remember to turn the fan on both at the switch on the wall and with the pull chain that hangs from it.

13. Once you've tested, turn the power back OFF. You want to finish the job without getting a shock.

14. Put the motor cover on over the motor and attach it with the screws provided. Tighten to make sure you have a good seal.

15. If you haven't done so already, attach each fan blade to its bracket. This is also where you are going to enlist your helper. The blades are usually large and a little awkward, so screwing them on is a little tricky.

16. Turn the power back on and test your work. Stand back, and test it on all settings. Does it make any strange noises? Is it off balance? Does it shake or wobble? If it doesn't hang quite straight, that is an easy

fix—just push it into place (make sure, of course, that the blades are not going at the time).

17. If the fan comes with a "balancing" kit, you can apply some of the tiny weights to the fan blades to allow them to balance. This is what they do when you get your tires balanced—they place small weights in your tire so that when it travels in a circular motion, it doesn't create vibrations and unsafe conditions. The same goes for your fan.

Tuff Tips

- If your fan has lights, the wall switch you hooked it up to will not work both the lights and the fan. Use the pull cords on the fan to adjust the lights and the speed of the fan. The wall switch will simply supply power to the unit.
- There are some ceiling fans out there that are controlled with a remote. Very handy!

Installing a Timer Switch

The easiest way I have found to install a timer switch is to buy the kind that plugs directly into the wall receptacle, and then plug the lamp directly into it. All you do is simply adjust the timer hands so the light comes on when you want it to. It's *so* easy! You will be surprised and proud of yourself after you take the couple of minutes to plug it in, set the timer, and then get the light you want *when* you want it.

Installing a Surge Protector

The "how to" on this one is pretty simple: buy a surge protector from your hardware store and plug it in! But wait—keep reading.

There is a wide range of quality and cost associated with surge protectors. You might not be fully aware of the compelling reasons why installing a quality surge protector is a must, so it's worth going into a little detail on the subject, especially if you do any work at home on a computer.

Lightning and power surges ruin computer equipment every day. And whether you've paid five hundred or five thousand dollars for your computer, you will want to protect your equipment, data, and hard work from being lost.

Power variances and surges pose a big threat to computer equipment, because the standard electricity coming from any utility company is rampant with irregularities and fluctuations. Electrical storms also pose a problem. While these fluctuations do not affect standard appliances such as lamps, digital clocks, and toasters, they can affect sensitive, intricate equipment like computers and televisions. Electrical storms and utility companies are not the only sources of power surges; old interior wiring is often a culprit. Even in buildings where the wiring is perfectly maintained, many everyday appliances like space heaters, microwaves, vacuum cleaners, and hair dryers can cause power overloads and surges, thus sending your treasures to an early demise.

The way to protect your computer and other electrical equipment from lightning and power surges is to use a good surge protector. First, it's easy to mistake a power strip for a surge protector. But they are different. A power strip is simply a row of outlets that allows you to plug more appliances into a single wall outlet. Power strips *can* include a surge protector—but not always. A surge protector may look like a power strip, but it has built-in protection against power surges.

When you go to buy a surge protector, carefully check all of the information on the box and talk to a hardware or electrical salesperson. The best surge protectors should offer the following features:

- Protection from lightning strikes
- Insurance to cover the loss of properly protected equipment
- Internet connection: Make sure you get a surge protector that is appropriate for your Internet connection. There are differences in protecting a dial-up modem and accommodating television/Internet cable.

When it comes to surge protection, you get what you pay for. Expect to pay thirty dollars or more for a quality surge protector.

Wattage Ratings

According to my mom, when I was growing up, I was always "working for the electric company." I didn't really understand what that meant until I was older—especially when I started paying my own electric bill. Since I was afraid of the dark, I was the queen of leaving all of the lights on in the house. Now I realize how important it is to save energy and turn off the lights—that one is easy. But I always wondered how the other appliances and electricity were used in my home, and therefore how they affected my electricity usage.

I've been on the road pretty solid now for three years, yet my electric bill is very large, whether I'm home or not. This got me wondering . . . why? Why, if I'm gone, all the lights are out, I'm not using any electronics, is it so much? After putting this list together, I discovered my main kWh culprit—my pool filter pump. I have since decreased the amount of time it runs per day, and have subsequently brought down my bill.

KILOWATT-HOURS USED PER MONTH

HOME SECTION	APPLIANCE	KWH USED PER MONTH
Kitchen—Small	Coffee maker	9
	Toaster	3
	Hand mixer	1
	Garbage disposal	3
	Deep fryer	7
	Frying pan	9
	Waffle iron	2
	Blender	<1
	Trash compactor	4
	Sandwich maker (grill)	3
	Hot plate	4
	Baby bottle warmer	2
Kitchen—Medium	Microwave oven	20
	Electric fryer	16
	Crock pot (slow cooker)	12
Kitchen—Large	Dishwasher	50
	Oven with range on top	30
	Self-cleaning oven w/range	102
	Refrigerator only—small	78
	Fridge/freezer combo	125

KILOWATT-HOURS USED PER MONTH

HOME SECTION	APPLIANCE	KWH USED PER MONTH
	Frost-free fridge/freezer	170
	Freezer only	135
	Frost-free freezer only	188
General house	Fan—circulating	4
	Fan—ceiling	12
	Fans—whole house	30
	Fan—attic	25
	Water heater (two people)	310
	Dehumidifier/humidifier	31
	Vacuum cleaner	8
	Sewing machine	1
	Clock radio	1
Office	Computer (desktop)	27
	Computer (laptop)	15
	Printer	5
	Scanner	5
	Router/Internet	5
Laundry	Dryer	75
	Washer	53
	Iron	9 *(cont.)*

KILOWATT-HOURS USED PER MONTH (CONT.)

HOME SECTION	APPLIANCE	KWH USED PER MONTH
Beauty	Curling iron/flat iron, etc.	7
	Hair dryer	10
	Hot rollers	7
	Electric razor	< ½
	Heating pad	15
	Electric toothbrush	< ½
Lighting	Inside: 4–5 rooms	50
	Inside: 6–8 rooms	60
	Outside: 1 light all night long	45
Home entertainment	TV (older models)	55
	TV (newer)	23
	Stereo	7
	CD/DVD player	9
Outside	Sprinkler system	28
	Pool pump	375
Seasonal	Heater	90
	Electric furnace	92
	Air conditioner (central air)	300
	A/C unit for one room	140
	Electric blanket	30

Electricity is measured in something called a kilowatt-hour, or kWh. How can we tell what a kWh is? It's about the equivalent of burning ten 100-watt lightbulbs for one hour (1,000 watts for one hour). We typically pay an electric bill monthly, so I have put together a list of common household items that we use, and typically how much kWh they use per month (on average). To find out how this translates in dollars, you will have to check with your local electric company, or review your bill, since electricity costs vary throughout the world.

There are several appliances now that list how many kWh they use per month and per year. The biggest difference one can make per year is a new energy-efficient refrigerator. With most other appliances, you can monitor how much you use them, and even cut back from time to time (like air-conditioning and heating, which are big kWh guzzlers), but a fridge stays on all the time. You don't have the option to turn it off and on. Older refrigerators take up the most electricity. When shopping for a new appliance, try to take into consideration how much electricity (and therefore) money you will save over the years, even if it's more expensive initially.

Keep in mind that these are merely averages. Of course, how much is really used in your own household is based on your own usage.

9

SECURITY AND SAFETY

We can be the Tuffest Chix on the planet, but that doesn't mean we're invincible. And it doesn't mean we need to take unnecessary risks. There is no good reason to ignore security, especially when most preventive measures are inexpensive and easy to take on your own.

Security is a way of safeguarding your home—but not just from unwanted visitors. There are many things in the home that are safety issues and therefore present a security problem for you and your loved ones. Safety is *such* an important topic, and it flows through to every aspect of home improvement.

But first, do you have an emergency plan? This includes being prepared for fire, earthquakes, tornadoes, hurricanes, or whatever other dangers exist in your area. Develop an emergency escape plan, and discuss it with all the members of your household. If you have children, develop a plan with them and practice it on a regular basis. Show them escape routes, teach them how to open (or even break) windows if necessary, and designate a meeting place outside.

Fire Prevention

We cannot talk about safety without mentioning fire prevention. Although we hear of forest fires all the time and feel helpless to make a difference in preventing them, most fires that occur in the home are caused by everyday items that most of us would consider safe. The best advice I can pass along is to use common sense and extreme care.

Fire extinguishers are a must. If you can't avoid a fire, this essential household item may turn out to be your best friend, but you should know when to use it and when it is better *not* to use it—and to run! First of all, keep a fire extinguisher in the kitchen, garage, and any other room that might present a fire hazard. When do you use one? When the fire is small and in a contained area, such as a kitchen, bathroom, laundry room, etc. When you see a large fire in a hallway, for instance, it's best to run and leave the extinguishing to the fire department.

PREVENTIVE MEASURES

Do all you can to keep fires from starting in the first place. Here's a list of preventive measures that will help reduce the risk of fire.

1. Appliances. Appliances of all shapes and sizes can put your household at risk for fire. Toasters, for example, tend to maintain their heat and are typically located in areas near towels or other combustible kitchen items. Larger appliances, too, such as clothes dryers and water heaters, require maintenance to avoid danger. Keep lint in both the lint screen and dryer duct hose (located in back) free of lint. Many times, clothes or towels can drop behind the dryer, creating a possible fire hazard. Keep all combustibles away from gas water heaters, as they may spark from time to time and cause a fire.

2. Kitchen and cooking fires. Be sure that curtains and other combustible materials are at least three feet away from the stovetop. Most kitchen fires start within the first fifteen minutes of cooking and usually happen in a pan. If a fire does start in a pan, just put a lid on it. Fire cannot live without oxygen, so give it a few minutes to put itself out. Many people tend to overreact and want to carry the fire out of the house. This, however, is very dangerous and can lead to an even bigger fire. Just imagine grabbing a pan full of flaming grease. You run

outside, spilling a little here and there on your wood floor or rug. This burning grease then lights up even more areas and you have yourself a full-blown house fire. Remember what I said about common sense? This is a prime example.

3. **Electrical fires.** Electrical fires happen fires when good cords go bad. Fire may be caused by old or worn extension cords, extension cord overload (plugging too many things into the same cord), damaged connections, or hidden electrical shorts. The use of oversized bulbs in light fixtures can also cause fire. When you purchase a new lamp be sure to read the instructions to determine the proper wattage for that particular fixture. Bulbs can range from 5 watts up to 1 million watts, but putting a 150-watt bulb into a 60-watt fixture can cause it to short, which may cause a fire. Examine your cords and replace any that are damaged, loose, or frayed. Make sure you are not using undersized cords, and that the extension cords are capable of handling the wattage you have plugged into them. If you are unsure, it is best to use a surge protector. If you are uncertain about the typical wattage of various appliances, check the "Wattage Ratings" chart on pages 218–220.

4. **Heating equipment.** This is the number one cause of household fires in America. Heating equipment includes, but is not limited to, space heaters, wood stoves, and the like. It also includes curling irons, ladies, so be sure to turn them off and unplug them before you leave the house. Keep curtains, drapes, and any other combustible materials at least three feet away from all heating equipment. Plug all heating equipment directly into the electrical socket. Do not use extension cords, since this can lead to unnecessary shorts, sparks, and fires. If you *must* use an extension cord, make sure it can handle the wattage. Buy good

quality extension cords. It's always better to buy the best than to lose everything in a fire.

5. Fireplaces and chimneys. All prevention manuals will tell you to keep a fire contained. What could be more contained than a fireplace? Why would a fireplace and chimney be cause for concern? Well, here's why. Ashes can stay hot and smolder for a couple of weeks. During a fire, and even after a fire, loose embers can rise from the chimney and start a blaze on any nearby brush. Often, debris from trees or bushes can fall into a chimney, catch fire, and venture out into the world. How to prevent this? Make sure you have your fireplace and chimney inspected and cleaned once a year. Make sure that the exterior of your chimney has a screen on top so that materials cannot easily fall into it. Keep all trees, branches, limbs, and bushes trimmed back away from the chimney. Inside, make sure drapes, curtains, rugs, and other combustible materials are at least three feet away from the fireplace, since sparks can fly in any direction. When you are done with a fire, you can clean up the ashes and store them in a covered steel container for a couple of weeks before discarding. Be sure the container is stored outside and away from combustible materials.

6. Smoking. Smoking not only kills people over time by causing lung cancer, it also kills people when smokers are careless. Often, people will fall asleep while smoking and drop a lit cigarette onto a bed or couch. Other times, smokers will not use a big enough ashtray and ashes will accumulate on a wood table or other combustible material. If you are a smoker, try to go outside to smoke, and use large ashtrays. If you are inside, use large ashtrays on tables and NEVER smoke in bed.

7. Candles. Feeling romantic? Candles are a perfect way to soften the mood, or even just to relax, but they are a common cause of many house fires. Always be sure to

keep combustible materials at least three feet away from the candle and, when possible, put the candle in a tip-proof container. Always use a plate or guard underneath a candle to prevent hot wax from dripping and starting a fire.

8. **Children.** Remember playing with fire when you were little? No? Well, I was a pyromaniac. I still love fire, though I'm now much safer about when and where I choose to enjoy a good blaze. A bonfire on the beach— it doesn't get much better than that. Mishaps with children and fire account for a little more that 5 percent of residential fires, and unfortunately, many of these mishaps result in death. Since children usually play with fire out of view of adults, there is a lot of potential for something to go wrong. Prevention is the key. Keep matches and lighters out of reach of children, and educate your kids about the dangers that accompany fires.

9. **Spontaneous combustion.** This is a concept that has fascinated and intrigued me over the years. According to Dictionary.com, the definition is: "Ignition of a substance, such as oily rags or hay, caused by a localized heat-increasing reaction between the oxidant and the fuel and not involving addition of heat from an outside source." And it's true! A pile of oil-soaked rags can generate enough heat simply to ignite—poof, up in flames. The concept is wild to me and hard for my little brain to understand, so I simply accept it. How do you prevent this? Spread out all rags containing any type of oil so that they can breath, cool down, and dry. Thus, no spontaneous fires.

INSTALLING SMOKE DETECTORS

If a fire starts in the night, the carbon monoxide produced by the smoke can make you go into a deeper sleep. A smoke detector can wake you up and save your life.

You may want to consider purchasing a combination smoke/carbon monoxide detector. They're more expensive (between thirty and seventy dollars), but well worth it—especially if your home is heated with gas or oil, or if you have an attached garage.

Most houses these days have smoke detectors, but the batteries in far too many are either dead or nonexistent. The first thing you should do—assuming you already have detectors—is light a match and test each alarm by blowing out the flame and letting smoke rise under the unit. Do this every year. Batteries should be tested every month and changed every six months. Detectors should also be cleaned regularly to get rid of dust (a vacuum cleaner works well), which can interfere with the operating system. Smoke detectors and alarms should be replaced roughly every ten years, although the quality of the product will play a role here.

Follow the installation and maintenance instructions carefully on all purchased detectors. The following general steps will help.

TUFF METER: 4

 TIMER: 30 minutes

TUFF TOOLS: Screwdriver, drill (depending on which detector you buy)

 SHOPPING LIST: Smoke detector kit ($12.49–$35)

 TOTAL PRICE: $12.49   **$95, plus materials**

How to install a smoke detector:

1. Walk through your home and locate the areas where you want to mount smoke detectors. In general, detectors should be placed inside bedrooms, just outside of bedrooms and in hallways leading to bedrooms. At least one should be placed on every level of the home, but they should *not* be mounted in kitchens and bathrooms (where smoke and steam can trigger the alarm) or in workshops or other places where fumes, dust, and smoke can set off a false alarm.

2. With a ladder, mount smoke detectors high on a wall or on the ceiling. Remember that smoke rises, so ceiling mounts will go off sooner and are therefore generally preferred.

3. If attaching a detector to a wall, place it 4–12 inches from the ceiling.

4. For ceiling detectors, measure at least 4 inches from the wall.

5. To prevent airflow from interfering with, or delaying, the alarm, position detectors away from windows and air-conditioning ducts.

6. In hallways, take care that the detectors are not placed too near bathroom doors. Steam from showers and baths can set off alarms.

7. Avoid corners; place detectors at least 12 inches away from them.

8. Follow the directions that come with your smoke detector kit. There are several ways in which detectors are installed, but all of them are fairly easy.

- Avoid basements and garages. Water heaters, dust, and fumes from solvents, paint, or gasoline can set off alarms.
- If you choose to go with a detector that will be hardwired to your home's electrical system, HAP (a qualified electrician).
- If your detector runs on batteries, replace the batteries when you change your clocks at the beginning and end of daylight saving time.

Security for the Home

Security is important for any family, but especially important for all you single women out there. When I first lived in Sherman Oaks, California, I was the victim of a break-in and assault. I lived with one other girl in a building that was built in the 1940s. The building was in a great area and was well kept, but the owners had replaced nothing. The windows were the old crank type, and did not provide a lot of security. I also lived on a busy street, and my windows were blocked by bushes and trees. Looking back now, the situation had all of the ingredients of a perfect target, but I was unaware of the potential dangers. I thought I was invincible—and besides, I lived in a great neighborhood, with nine other units that constantly had people milling about.

One night, I came home at about 10 P.M. to a dark house.

My roommate had left only fifteen minutes before. A friend walked me to the door, made sure I got inside, made me lock the door and put on the chain, and yelled good-bye as he headed back to his car. I yelled good-bye back to him, with my lips pressed up against the doorjamb. It was then that I heard Mercury (my kitty) meow this meow that I had never heard before, nor have to this day. It was a deep, scared, warning meow. I turned around, and there was a man standing in my hallway. He headed toward me, told me not to scream, and threw me up against the wall. He calmly unlatched the chain, unlocked the deadbolt, and walked out the front door, in front of several of my neighbors.

I gathered myself for a moment, and by the time I got up and started screaming, he was long gone. My neighbors came over, we called the police, but he was never found. He entered through the kitchen window, and left through the front door.

MAKE YOUR HOME A BAD TARGET

So why was my apartment such a good target? Several reasons—things you can check out in your own home, to make sure this doesn't happen to you.

1. My apartment was dark. There were no motion-sensitive lights in either the front or the back of the unit. A burglar had plenty of time to go unnoticed in the darkness. **Recommendation:** Install motion-sensitive light around the entire perimeter of your house or apartment. I now have them everywhere. Once in a while they'll go on due to a neighborhood critter, but I'd much rather have the lights go on occasionally than have them stay off when a burglar is around!

2. My windows were easy to open. The old crank-style windows are easy to pull open. Once you have it open just a few inches, a burglar can reach in and crank the

window the rest of the way. We also had no additional safety locks on any of the windows. **Recommendation:** Replace the windows with sturdier windows. If you do not have the financial means to replace windows, find sturdy locks for whatever type of window you have. Keep broom sticks in sliding glass doors.

3. Although I lived on a busy street, my windows were hidden by overgrown brush and trees. Even if cars drove by slow enough to notice, drivers would never have seen through the brush. **Recommendation:** Trim all bushes and trees so that your windows are visible. This will also help if you should ever need to evacuate your home through a window.

4. My door was equipped with a dead bolt and a chain. Although he did not break in through the door, I realized that these were both weak attempts at locks. The strike plate (the stationary metal plate that meets up with the deadbolt in the doorjamb) was held to the jamb with short screws, as was the chain attachment. One good kick and those tiny screws would have given way. **Recommendation:** Strike plates and chain attachments should be put on with long screws, to give the lock some leverage and allow it to do its job properly (see p. 123). Also, buy sturdy locks. They are more expensive, but not by much. I'd rather spend a little extra money to ensure that my home, my possessions, and most importantly, my family is safe. It's a small price to pay. Also, make sure your exterior doors are not made of hollow wood or composite material. Make sure they are steel, fiberglass, or solid wood.

Although implementing these recommendations may not have kept me burglar free forever, they certainly would have acted as a deterrent. If any one aspect of this list had been present, it's likely he would not have had the time to break in, and I would have been inside before him, thus encouraging him to go away. Remember, my roommate had only left minutes before.

OTHER SECURITY CONCERNS

Most burglaries happen when people are at work, between 8 A.M. and 5 P.M. Oftentimes, burglars will pose as a moving company, with a fake business name on the side of a truck or merely a large rental truck, and will take everything you own. When I was young, a moving truck pulled up to our neighbor's home and began packing up. They were not sneaky or trying to be inconspicuous, merely going about their business. My mom thought it was strange, since we did not see a For Sale sign, but they looked legitimate. Unfortunately, we did not have our neighbors' work number to give them a call. To our horror (and theirs), they came home to an empty house. The burglars had taken everything—in the middle of the day. **Recommendation:** Lock all doors and windows, even if you are just going out for a little while during the day. Also, get involved with your neighborhood watch program. That way, your neighbors will know when you are moving, and to call the police if there is any unexplained "moving" activity. Get alternate numbers for your neighbors, and alert them if anything looks suspicious.

Keep tools and ladders inside a locked garage. Many times, thieves will look in someone's own garage to gain an advantage. Imagine—someone using your tools against you! If they find a ladder, they can access a second-story window with ease, which is usually more likely to be left open.

Some of the more high-tech thieves will uses devices to open automatic garage doors. Buy a garage door remote with built-in security, or change your code from time to time. Be sure to lock the door in your garage that accesses your home. Just because it is inside a garage, does not mean that it is safe.

SECURITY SYNOPSIS

1. Lock your house, even if you are just going out for a minute.

2. Install sturdy strike plates and door chains with long screws.

3. Clear overgrown brush from around the house, especially near windows.

4. Buy sturdy exterior doors.

5. Install motion-sensitive lights around the perimeter of your home.

6. Add lights around your home.

7. Keep ladders and tools locked inside the home or garage.

8. Change garage remote codes often.

Lights, Camera—Safety!

As I've said before, lighting is so important. It greets you when you come home and wards off unfriendly visitors. Adding general lighting, motion sensors, and timers will not only improve the look of your home, it will provide extra security. Please turn to the electrical chapter of this book for further information on lighting and the basics of electrical repair.

Installing lights, or switching existing light fixtures for time and/or motion sensitivity, is often a simple procedure in itself, but there are a few things to consider, in addition to safety, *before* buying lights and deciding where to put them.

Effective (and legal!) lighting design should incorporate energy efficiency, environmental factors (such as sky glow or impact on local wildlife), and the requirements of indoor and outdoor lighting codes.

Follow the National Electrical Code when installing any lighting, and check for local government regulations as well. Outdoor lights trespassing onto adjacent properties is a common mistake. When your security light effectively lights up your entire neighborhood, it could be a problem.

How about a security camera? If you have the means to HAP, I would suggest it. Sometimes even just the appearance of a camera will be enough to ward off any unfriendly visitors.

ADDING SECURITY LIGHTING

Here are a few things to keep in mind when adding security-oriented lighting:

1. Light sources ideal for motion sensors include fluorescent and induction lamps. (Induction lamps are fairly new to the market and more expensive than other light sources, but because they have a light bulb with no filament or electrodes, they have incredibly long lives, and hence virtually zero maintenance costs. They are also good for cold climates.)

2. When using "on/off" motion sensors for security lighting, avoid the lights that take a while to light up completely. (This includes high-intensity discharge, or HID, sources such as metal halide or high-pressure sodium. HID lights are popular for lighting indoor spaces with high ceilings.) Incandescent sources (essentially your regular lightbulb) are the best for this type of application since they will be on for a limited time and are not sensitive to temperature effects. Plus, when you have an intruder, you want to light them up as soon as possible—urging them to leave.

ADDING MOTION SENSORS

The best way to install a motion-sensitive external light is to add a motion sensor to an existing external light (such as a floodlight in the backyard).

TUFF METER: 4

TIMER: 1 hour

TUFF TOOLS: Screwdriver, drill

SHOPPING LIST: Motion sensor ($16.99–$93.89)

TOTAL PRICE: $16.99

$95, plus materials

How to install an external motion sensor:

1. Turn off the power at the main circuit breaker or fuse box.

2. Remove the existing light by unscrewing it and pulling it out. You will then need to unscrew the wire nuts. Be sure to note which wires went where, although they should be color coded. If the wires were held together with tape, unravel the tape and purchase wire nuts. They provide a much better seal, especially for outdoor applications.

3. Follow the manufacturer's instructions, since many motion sensors have different requirements.

4. Attach the motion sensor to the light and connect the wires to the corresponding wires with wire nuts. Be sure to screw the wire nuts on tight for a good connection.

5. Reattach the light to its base by screwing it back on.

6. To be sure that you have installed it correctly, give it a test run. Typically, the manufacturer's instructions will tell you to turn off the wall switch, wait ten seconds, and then turn it on again.

7. You can often adjust the motion sensors, as well. Options include adjusting the light to point to where you want it, adjusting how long the light will stay on when tripped, and adjusting the sensitivity (range).

Doors: Security and Safety

SLIDING GLASS DOORS

It's easy to strengthen the security of your sliding doors. On the bottom track, simply lay a cut-to-fit piece of wood inside the track. You can get this at any hardware store. You can also use a broom handle.

Make sure your sliding glass doors are correctly installed. If you do not have a track on the inside where you can put such a homemade security device, change the tracks. This is a bit of a difficult job and I would suggest HAP.

The block or broom handle stops an intruder from entering your home through the sliding glass door, but does not prevent breakage. If a criminal is determined enough, he will find a way to break the glass. Most intruders will not, however, because it causes a tremendous amount of noise.

But enough about intruders. What about the people living in your home and using the sliding doors on a daily basis? Well, there is a way to make them safer for them, too.

We've all seen the commercial with the birds that try to fly into someone's house and hit the glass instead. Although it's a cute advertisement for a window cleaner, it's not so cute when you have a real bird or bigger bird (such as a friend or a child) attempt the very same thing. When my brother was in high school, he made the unfortunate mistake of running into a (very clean) sliding glass door at a friend's house. The glass broke and he was left holding two very large glass shards in his hands. Although not seriously hurt, he sliced both palms and took a trip to the emergency room. If those glass shards had landed elsewhere, or he had been smaller, it might have resulted in serious injury—even death.

Manufacturers today are very aware of the safety issues glass presents and have worked to combat the problem is two ways: tempered glass and laminated glass. Tempered glass shatters into thousands of tiny little pieces. Because of this shattering effect, there are no large pieces of glass that can become razors or guillotines. Laminated glass works in the opposite way but achieves the same result. The glass is covered with a film that holds it together (kind of like on a car windshield), so that no large shards can do any damage.

If your glass is older, you may want to consider strengthening the glass and making it safer by a process called "safety glazing," which involves putting a filmlike laminating coat over the glass and is not really visible to the eye. You can purchase glazing materials that will help minimize injury (and even death) should the glass break. You can find out more information on-line by looking up the Safety Glazing Certification Council (SGCC).

EXTERIOR DOORS

Here are some ways to help secure your doors:

1. You may want to think about adding a peephole and/or a dead bolt to your front door for extra security (see p. 115 and p. 124).

2. Make sure your doors are not hollow, and avoid doors with glass panels. The glass may be prettier, but definitely is not the safest option. The best doors are made of steel or solid wood.

3. If you do have glass anywhere on a door, make sure it is safety glass. If it's not, you can add a layer of plastic film as discussed in the previous section.

4. Exterior doors should have dead bolts. Stay away from simply having doorknobs with a lock on the inside of them.

5. Do not use doorknobs that have keyed locks on both sides of them. This will make it very difficult to use the door as an escape route.

Windows: Security and Safety

Windows protect our home from the elements, brighten every room, and provide a nice view to the outdoors. Windows can be a source of tragedy, however. Children fall from windows many times each year, resulting in injury and sometimes death. The saddest part about this is that *it can be avoided*!

See the following section below about how to childproof your home.

Like sliding glass doors, windows can also be made stronger with tempering, laminating, or glazing. Many new windows come with "impact-resistance" ratings. With all of the hurricanes we have had lately, it makes sense to have windows that will not become weapons if they are broken in extreme weather conditions. There is now also glass that is so resistant, it will not break if hit with a baseball bat. Believe me—I've tried! You can beat it and beat it, and eventually it will shatter, but it will stay in the frame, making life *very* difficult for an intruder. After the first few blows, he will probably give up and find an easier target.

There are several window locks on the market that are easy to install and that will help to deter intruders. Make sure that they are easy for you to unlock should an emergency (like a fire) occur.

Your windows can either be your escape route or the reason you perish in a house fire. Look at all of your windows in the house. Make sure they can all be opened. If they are painted over or nailed shut, you will not be able to get out in time. Remove any nails or screws that are holding a window shut. Take a utility knife and break the seal if a window has been painted shut. Make sure that windows are not blocked by air-conditioning units. If you have one unit in a window, make sure there is an alternate window in the same room that can be used as an escape route.

Childproofing

An estimated 2.5 million children are injured or killed by hazards in the home each year.* Here's the good news: You can childproof your home for a fraction of what it would cost to have a professional do it. And safety devices are easy to find. You can buy them at hardware stores, baby stores, supermarkets, drug stores, home and linen stores, and through mail-order catalogues.

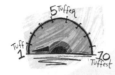

TUFF METER: 1

TIMER: Depends how much you want to secure!

TUFF TOOLS: Screwdriver, drill

SHOPPING LIST: Any items you wish to secure your house with

TOTAL PRICE: Safety latch or lock ($2), safety gate ($13–$40), doorknob cover ($1), door lock ($5 and up), window guard or safety netting ($8–$16), corner and edge guards ($1 and up), outlet cover ($2)

$50/hour, plus materials

How to childproof your home:

1. Use safety latches and locks for cabinets and drawers in kitchens, bathrooms, garages, tool rooms, and any

---

* U.S. Consumer Product Safety Commission, "Childproofing Your Home." http://www.cpsc.gov.

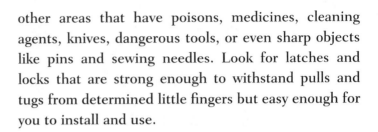

other areas that have poisons, medicines, cleaning agents, knives, dangerous tools, or even sharp objects like pins and sewing needles. Look for latches and locks that are strong enough to withstand pulls and tugs from determined little fingers but easy enough for you to install and use.

2. Install doorknob covers and door locks to keep children out of rooms that could present even the chance of an accident, including garages and swimming pools. For pools, gate and door locks should be placed as high up as is practical. Be especially wary of sliding glass doors leading to pools: locks that must be resecured after each entry or exit are *not* ideal.

3. Install safety gates to stop young children from falling down stairs and to keep them away from dangerous areas. When you want to block off stairs, look for safety gates that screw to the wall, since these are much harder to dislodge than "pressure gates." New safety gates that comply with national standards will have a certification seal from the Juvenile Products Manufacturers Association (JPMA). If you have an older safety gate, make sure the spaces between the bars are too small for a child to squeeze his or her head through.

3. Use corner and edge guards or bumpers to cushion falls. Look for guards that stay securely attached.

4. Buy outlet covers for electrial receptacles. These are the plastic inserts that fit directly into the receptacles. Use these to help prevent electrocution and electric shock. Make sure they cannot be easily removed by children and that they are too big for a child to swallow.

5. Install a lid lock for toilets. Many children are curious and unfortunately drown in toilets by falling in after lifting the lid.

6. Install guards and safety netting to keep children falling from decks and balconies. There should be no more than four inches between the bars of the guard.

7. Windows:

   a. Watch your children at all times when around open windows. It only takes a second for a child to get curious, poke his head out the window, and fall. Better yet, keep windows closed when children are present.

   b. If you want a window open for ventilation, only open it a crack and wedge something in the jamb so it cannot be opened more. Even a five-inch gap can pose a problem! Also, try cracking a window that is out of the child's reach.

   c. Children are crafty! Make sure to keep all furniture they could climb on away from windows.

   d. Window screens are really good at keeping critters out, but *not* effective for keeping children in. A screen will do *nothing* to prevent a child from falling out a window. You can install window guards, but make sure that they have a quick-release mechanism, so that in a fire, you can easily escape. Before you install window guards, check your local building codes.

   e. The best plan: common sense. Talk to your kids about the potential dangers that windows provide. Teach them not to go near them or to play near them.

Tuff Tip

Using a cordless phone will make it easier to keep an eye on young children, especially when they're in the bath, swimming pool, or other potentially dangerous areas.

Garage Door Sensors

Most new automatic garage doors come with sensors attached to the bottom of the door opening. If you are purchasing an automatic garage door, be sure that it has these sensors. The sensors will not allow the garage door to close if something is in the way. This is especially critical for children and pets.

When I was in grade school, Licorice (my nine-year-old kitty, and therefore part of the family) met her maker by trying to squeeze through the old garage door. If we had sensors, Licorice might still be with us today.

Mold and Rot Prevention

Mold, a safety issue? Yes! Mold can make you sick. Many factors can lead to mold and rot, which can in turn lead to serious problems both for your home and for your family members living in the home. Mold and rot are usually caused by excessive moisture and insufficient ventilation. What are the potential sources of moisture? Here are some things to look for and avoid: leaks anywhere (including various pipes, the roof, the foundation), interior dampness or humidity, flooding or puddling of water. All of these factors can contribute to mold.

How do you determine if you have mold? Look under flooring, wallpaper, and carpet in likely damp areas for black dots. If you are still unsure, call your local health department and ask for mold-testing advice. You can also call a mold inspection company to come to your home; however, this can get very costly just for a visit, and abatement (removal) is extremely expensive.

Most of the mold found in the home is surface mold and/or mildew. Surface mold grows in any damp location and can look like black dots, white scum, or a gooey discoloration. To remove surface mold or mildew, scrub the surface with a strong mildew cleanser. If you don't have a strong cleanser, detergent or dish soap will also work. Always remember to keep the area clean and dry. Before you clean, be sure to protect yourself. Mildew and mold are not good for the human lungs and can cause allergic reactions. Wear a long-sleeved shirt, pants, goggles, and gloves. If the cleanser you are using is particularly strong, you should use a face mask (or dust mask). If you scrub continuously and mold is still visible, cover it with your cleanser and let it sit for a couple of hours and scrub again. Be sure to keep the area well ventilated. Many times mildew may accumulate around tile and in grout. Once you have the area cleaned and dry, apply a couple of coats of sealer. This will keep mildew and mold from accumulating as much in the future; plus, it will contain the mold to the surface rather than allowing it to burrow deep inside your home.

Here are some places in the home you are likely to find mold:

1. Bathroom: The area surrounding the toilet is the most likely place to find mold. Try to rock your toilet back and forth. If it doesn't move, you are in good shape. If it does move, you may have a problem. This usually means that the wax ring under the toilet is not getting a tight seal and may be leaking. This is an easy fix. Refer to the section of this book on toilets (p. 188). The second most likely place to find mold is around the walls of the shower or on the floor near the tub. Make sure that the caulking is in good shape, and not turning dark. If it is, it's an easy fix. Just refer to the section on recaulking (p. 51).

2. Laundry room: Check the hoses to your washer to make sure there is a tight connection. It's a good idea

to install a watertight pan to catch overflows so water doesn't leak and find it's way to the walls.

3. **Foundation:** You always want to keep your house's foundation dry. If drainage is poor around house, it will lead to a damp foundation, creating more problems than just mold. Make sure the soil around the house slopes away from house so that water can drain away from, not toward, the foundation.

4. **Exteriors:** The exterior of your home is what protects you and your family, so it's best to start here. Clogged or leaky gutters can lead to excessive moisture on the home. Missing or worn-out shingles allow water to leak through to the attic and soak into the roof's edge, making a very damp situation that is difficult to dry. If you see peeling paint on any part of the house (siding, soffit, fascia), you may encounter moisture problems. Another key to keeping moisture away is simply having good ventilation in the attic. That way, even if there are the occasional mishaps, they won't become full-blown problems.

5. **Windows:** Water can accumulate around windowsills or may even penetrate through cracks or bad seals. Decay around windowsills is a common problem. This is where you are likely to see rot. Water gets in, and although you would expect the sun to dry it, warmth from the sun can actually push moisture deep into the wood. Once decay has set in, it creates future problems. Damaged wood is more porous and can work like a sponge, soaking up water faster in the future, much faster than solid wood. The best way to combat this problem is to scrape off chipping or flaking paint and either apply a wood preservative or a new coat of paint. Recaulk around the windowsill to assure that there is a good seal. If you have condensation on the inside of your windows, it is the sign of a problem. You can use a

dehumidifier to take out some of the moisture for short-term relief. If you have the means, it is best to get more efficient windows.

6. **Doors:** Water can accumulate around doors, especially where the door doesn't meet up properly with the doorjamb. Heavy rain or sprinkler runoff can get under the door and soak into the floorboards. Rain can also affect the size of the door, since it will swell or shrink according to the weather. The best way to combat this problem is to assure that the door is properly equipped with weather stripping. Weather stripping is the lining around your doors that prevents drafts and leaks from entering your home. Check to make sure it is not rotting, dry, cracked, or flaking and is securely in place. Although the stripping may appear to be in good shape, it still may not be laid correctly (see p. 112). Make sure it makes a good seal.

10

ORGANIZING AND SPACE SAVING

There's probably a lot more space in your closets, your garage, and other storage areas than you realize. And there's a good chance a lot of the space is wasted. It's likely wasted in two ways: (1) cluttered up by stuff you don't really need and should get rid of, and (2) cluttered by bad organization and poorly designed spaces.

A good space-saving and organizing mission has to start with getting rid of all that stuff you don't need. It's hard, but like a good workout—*so* worth it! Donate it to a charity, have a garage sale, or just use a good old-fashioned trash can. Doing this before you put up shelves or rods or reorganize entire closets will make your life much easier!

There are lots of different ways to better organize space and lots of companies, kits, and gadgets out there to help. Different projects will suit different needs, but some of my favorites follow.

Installing Shelves in Your Garage

Who doesn't need more room to put belongings in the garage? Even if you pride yourself on being an anti-junk queen, and guard against accumulating stuff in the same way you guard against accumulating calories, it's always satisfying to make an existing space work better for you and to better organize the things you do decide to keep and store.

Putting up shelves can be one of those jobs that's not *really* that difficult, but it does take effort and skill. Believe me, though, you'll feel pleased with yourself when you're done.

Tuff Tips

- For the garage, buy laminated shelves (particleboard with plastic laminate). These shelves are resistant to paint, gas, or oil spillages and clean very easily. They are also very sturdy. Sure, they are not the prettiest, but for the garage, they are perfect.
- Always put shelves up on studs. If you cannot find adequate anchors in one particular area, use wall anchors and be sure not to overload the area.

TUFF CHIX DICTIONARY

Brackets: Angled strips of metal or wood with slots that anchor shelves.

Wall anchors: You can buy plastic or metal versions of these (use metal for thicker walls). After you've drilled a hole in the wall, anchors are inserted into the hole. They are designed to expand and hold the screw securely. You should only use these if you are unable to locate a stud in the area.

BRacket

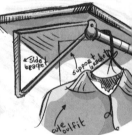

side bracket

support bracket

cute outfit

TUFF METER: 5

TIMER: 30 minutes

TUFF TOOLS: Power drill (with screwdriver bit), hammer, measuring tape, level, ⅛-inch drill bit

SHOPPING LIST: Shelves ($14.99), brackets ($6.99), wall anchors and screws ($1.86–$4.07/box). Or you can buy shelves that come with everything you need.

TOTAL PRICE: $23.84

$20/hour, plus materials

How to install shelves:

1. Hold one of the shelf brackets against the wall to measure how far you want the shelf to be from the ceiling or the floor, and mark the spot for the top and bottom of each bracket with a pencil.

SAFETY: Safety eyewear should be worn.

2. Measure the length of the shelf to see how far apart the brackets should be.

3. Locate and mark the wall studs (see p. 265) These are where you will put your brackets for your shelves.

4. Use a level to make sure each bracket is level both horizontally and vertically. With a pencil, mark inside each bracket hole where you will need to drive your screw.

5. Remove the bracket from the wall. Use a drill with a screwdriver attachment to drill tiny little pilot holes in the spots you've marked, with the $1/8$-inch drill bit.

6. Hold the bracket in place over the pilot holes and double-check to make sure it's level and plumb (straight, vertically). Then insert the screws through the bracket slots and into the studs. Screw them tightly into place with the drill.

7. Double-check the spacing between the brackets. (You can hold the shelf up and get a helper to mark the spot, or just use a tape measure.) Repeat step 6 to install the second bracket.

8. Place the shelf on the brackets.

Tuff Tip

When using a drill with a screwdriver attachment to drive in a screw, use a sleeve cover (personally, one of my favorite inventions). This slides down over the screw, keeping it from swirling and getting away from you.

These days, there are plenty of companies that will come in and organize your closets for you—whether it's building shelves, drawers, boxed spaces, a closet, or even constructing an entire walk-in wardrobe. These companies can do a glamorous job, but as with many of the best things in life, you'll pay for it!

In almost every bedroom or storage room (and certainly any home office), space can be used more wisely by putting up shelves, adding an extra rod in your existing closet, or making special storage spaces for shoes, hats, and folded clothes.

If you don't want to hire a professional (HAP), below are some basic DIY jobs that will help you to make better use of your space. Unless you're comfortable with cutting your own shelves from scratch, you will need to measure your closet space and take those measurements to your hardware store, or get online and check out the various closet-organizer kits on the market, which start at around thirty dollars.

Tuff Tip

A low shelf just five inches off the floor and the width of the closet will make an efficient space for shoes.

PUTTING SHELVES IN YOUR CLOSET

TUFF METER: 5

TIMER: 30 minutes

TUFF TOOLS: Pry bar, power drill (with screwdriver bit), hammer, measuring tape, level, pencil

SHOPPING LIST: Shelves ($14.99), brackets ($6.99), or a closet organizer kit ($19.99–$189)

TOTAL PRICE: $21.98 or $19.99–$189 for an organizer kit $20/hour, plus materials

How to put up shelves in your closet:

1. Measure the width, depth, and height of your closet, and take those measurements to your hardware store to make sure you buy the right-sized shelving. You can buy premade shelves that come with brackets or buy raw wood that is cut to size and purchase brackets.

2. If you have existing shelving that you want to take down, remove any existing brackets, and use a crowbar to loosen and remove the support boards for the old shelves. Remove any old nails with the forked end of your hammer.

3. Follow the directions on page 255 for installing shelves.

4. If you've bought an organizing kit, and not just shelves, build the rest of the kit according to the manufacturer's directions. (Most organizers have a core section that must be assembled, with a couple of fixed shelves, but the other parts can often be assembled in a variety of ways.)

ADDING A CLOTHES ROD

An easy way to double the hanging space in your closet is to add an extra rod. There are cheap "add-a-rod" solutions available in hardware stores and on-line, which simply hook over your existing rod (they range from slick-looking metal and wooden rods to cheap plastic hooks) and give you another, lower-level hanging space.

Another solution is to add a more permanent rod either beside your existing rod, or lower down in the closet for hanging shorter clothes.

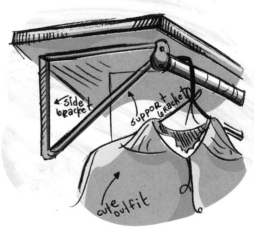

TUFF METER: 5

 TIMER: 30 minutes

TUFF TOOLS: Crowbar, power drill (with screwdriver bit), hammer, measuring tape, level, pencil, ⅛-inch drill bit

SHOPPING LIST: Rod ($1.39/sq. ft.), brackets ($6.99), wood screws ($1.89–$4.07), support bracket (if needed; $2.95)

TOTAL PRICE: $20.20 (for 6-foot rod)

$20/hour, plus materials

How to hang a clothes rod:

1. Using your clothes to judge the best height for a second rod, mark the correct place on the closet wall for the rod sockets, keeping about 12 inches from the back of the closet.

2. With a measuring tape, carefully measure the height and depth of the place marked so you can make a mark in the same place on the opposite wall assuring your rod will be straight.

3. Hold the closet rod sockets in the places you have marked, first one side, then the other, and mark where you will need to drill holes to attach the screws. (One-inch screws will usually do the job here, but check with your hardware salesperson when you purchase the rod kit and/or brackets.)

4. Screw the rod brackets in, according to the manufacturer's instructions.

5. If one bracket is a complete circle, with no space left open to drop in the rod, put the rod in that side first. The other bracket should have an opening the size of the rod. Hang your new rod by simply dropping it into the bracket.

6. If the rod spans more than four feet, you will need to install a support bracket in the middle. This might be a good idea even if the rod is smaller than 4 feet, if you plan to hang heavy clothes on the rod.

Adding a support bracket:

1. Buy a support bracket at the hardware store. These are usually white-painted metal.

2. Measure the size of the opening spanned by the rod. On the back wall, mark the center of the span. Check to make sure that this mark aligns with a stud. If it

does, you are ready to go. If it does not, you will need to adjust the measurement slightly to the right or the left until you find a stud. It is *very* important that the support bracket is screwed into a stud. This will give it the "support" it needs to be a proper support bracket.

3. Hold the bracket up to the wall and align the top of the support bracket with the circular rod brackets to make sure they are at the same level.

4. Mark the openings in the support bracket with a pencil.

5. Remove the bracket from the wall. Use a drill with a screwdriver attachment to drill tiny little pilot holes in the spots you've marked, with a ⅛-inch drill bit.

6. Hold the bracket in place over the pilot holes and double-check to make sure it's level and plumb (straight, vertically). Then insert the screws through the bracket slots and into the studs. Screw them tightly into place with the drill.

Repairing a clothes rod. If you need to repair a clothes rod, see where the repairs need to be made and follow the directions listed above to replace the broken parts. Usually, the brackets have cracked or broken because they are made out of plastic. Buy replacement brackets or rods or support brackets and get to work. If you want added support, buy wood or metal brackets.

Hiding Those Unsightly Power Cords

One trick I like is to buy a cute hatbox or leather box, cut a hole in it, and feed all those ugly electrical cords into it. There are also a bunch of specially designed electrical accessories for doing the same thing—streamlining, hiding, and decorating. Take a look at the hardware store or at an office supply store.

11

HANG IT UP

There are always things around the house that need hanging up: shower curtains, miniblinds, curtain rods, pictures, mirrors—the list goes on and on. If you understand the basics, you can tackle just about any project.

The first thing to understand: studs. No, not tall, dark, handsome men, but the wood braces that hold up your home. These are what you need to hammer into to properly hang something on drywall. They give you the stability and safety you need.

To help with hanging objects on the wall, you might want to get a "stud finder." This can be purchased at any hardware store and ranges in price. It will be key in helping you hang things on the wall.

Shower Curtain and Rod

Here is a project where you won't need to worry about finding any studs: the shower curtain. The shower curtain is such a simple thing, yet it provides a much-needed barrier, keeping water from the shower out of the rest of the bathroom. They come in a variety of styles and materials—which one you choose is completely up to you.

Shower curtains are inexpensive and easy to hang. You can get shower rods that require drilling into the tile, but I suggest getting a telescopic shower curtain rod. This uses a simple, spring-loaded mechanism to hold the rod in place between two walls.

Buy a tension or telescopic rod and follow the manufacturer's directions, which tend to vary. Make sure you measure the opening you need to span, and buy the corresponding rod. There is usually a range, so make sure your buy the right one. Typically, you will put the shower curtain on the rod when it is down, and then simply hold it in place and expand the rod until it's tight and snug.

Window Coverings

Window coverings not only add to the look and style of the home, they also provide privacy, safety, and way to stay asleep in the mornings. And, the best part about window coverings is that they are easy to install.

There are several different types of window coverings, including blinds, curtains, shades, and shutters. Picking the right kind for you and your space is completely up to you.

SHUTTERS

I believe that shutters definitely look the best in a home, but they are *very* expensive. I would not attempt to install them. You are looking to HAP if you want these babies in your home.

BLINDS

Blinds are a much more economical way to go and can end up giving you the same feel as shutters. They come in many sizes and variations, and can be made from vinyl, plastic, aluminum, or wood. There are vertical blinds and horizontal blinds. My favorite are the three-inch faux-wood blinds. They give the look of expensive wooden blinds at a fraction of the cost.

You can mount blinds on the outside of the window frame (the trim surrounding the window) or on the inside of the frame. It is up to you, and the mounting brackets that come with the blinds will usually determine which you want to do.

To buy the correct size, first decide if you want to put your blinds outside or inside the frame. Measure the width of the window, inside the frame. Because our homes are not perfect, it's a good idea to measure across the top, the middle, and the bottom. Use your smallest measurement to proceed. Now measure the height. You do not have to be as specific with the height, since you will most likely have to shorten the blinds to fit your needs, unless you custom order them. Directions for cutting the length will be provided by the manufacturer. You will want your blinds to rest gently on the sill.

What about studs? Since window frames are entirely built out of two-by-fours, you are surrounded by studs! No need to worry.

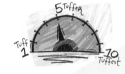

TUFF METER: 5

TIMER: 1 hour

TUFF TOOLS: Pencil, drill with ⅛-inch drill bit (for pilot holes) and screwdriver attachment, screwdriver

SHOPPING LIST: Blinds ($13.99–$29.99 and up)

TOTAL PRICE: $13.99

$30/window, plus materials

How to install blinds:

1. Decide where you want to position the blinds at the top of the window. Mark the position with a pencil. You will want them to be about ½ inch down from the top of the frame if you are mounting inside. If you are mounting outside, you must make sure that you position the blinds close enough to the window that you still drill

into the studs. Mark where you want your mounting brackets to go.

2. Take your mounting brackets and hold them up to your markings. Make sure you have the correct one for each side (they should be marked left and right). Mark through the holes to indicate where you will place your mounting screws.

3. Drill pilot holes through these marks for the mounting screws.

4. Using the screws provided, install the mounting brackets with either a screwdriver or a drill with a screwdriver attachment.

5. Install the blinds by putting the top bar into the brackets. Close the bracket to ensure the blind stays in place.

6. If needed, cut the length of the blind according to the manufacturer's instructions.

CURTAINS

Curtains are a great way to add security and privacy, and to keep out unwanted sunlight while providing an elegant look to any room. Just adding or changing drapery can add so much to the look and feel of your home. During the day you can open them and let in the sunlight. And at night, you can pull them closed and use them to shelter you from the morning sun when you sleep in.

What about studs?

Yes, here is a project that *definitely* requires you to attach to a stud. Break out that stud finder and mark where the studs are.

TUFF METER: 5

TIMER: 1 hour

TUFF TOOLS: Pencil, drill with ⅛-inch drill bit (for pilot holes) and screwdriver attachment, screwdriver, level

SHOPPING LIST: Curtain rod, curtains ($2.99–$59 and up)

TOTAL PRICE: Varies

$30/rod, plus materials

How to hang a curtain rod:

1. Decide where you want your curtains to go. They are typically set about 3 inches above the window frame, but looking around my house, they are 6–8 inches above my windows. Have a friend hold up the rod with curtains on it to see what looks best. Horizontally, it is best to position them about 3–6 inches beyond the edge of the window frame. The decision as to whether you want them to hang above the floor or puddle at the bottom is personal, and should match the style of your home. Remember, look for the studs.

2. Mark where you want the rod to go. Use a level to assure that it is even on both sides. Keep in mind your markings for the studs.

3. Take the brackets and hold them up to your markings. Making sure they are lined up on studs, mark with a pencil the area you will be placing the screws that come with the rod.

4. If your rod is longer than 4 feet, you will need to attach a central support bracket, which should come with the rod. You will need to install this on a stud as well.

5. Drill pilot holes into the wall and stud with the ⅛-inch drill bit.

6. Holding the bracket up to the wall with the holes over your pilot holes, insert the screws into the pilot holes. You can use a screwdriver or drill with a screwdriver attachment to tighten them.

7. Put the curtains on the curtain rod.

8. Put the rod into the brackets and adjust the curtains.

Hanging a Picture or Mirror on Drywall

Pictures, art, and mirrors definitely add to the beauty and style of the home. Plus, they allow a relatively inexpensive way to change your decor without changing too much—you can simply switch a painting.

Depending on the weight of the picture you intend to hang, you will need to find the studs. If you have something that is really light, it is okay to take a small nail and simply tap it into the drywall. But if you are hanging something that weighs over one pound, it is best to find a stud.

Manufacturers have made specialized drywall hanging kits, which include a combination of nail and hook that can withstand a significant amount of weight. When you buy such a kit, be sure to check how much it will safely hold. In my opinion, it's always best to find a stud.

TUFF METER: 1

TIMER: 20 minutes

TUFF TOOLS: Pencil, hammer, level

SHOPPING LIST: Picture-hanging nails ($1.99–$3.99) or picture-hanging kit ($2.69/4-pack)

TOTAL PRICE: $1.99   **$20/hour**

How to hang a picture or mirror on drywall:

1. First decide where on the wall you would like your picture to go. Mark the spot lightly with a pencil.

2. Find the stud nearest to that area.

3. On that stud, hold the picture up again to get the designated height. With a mirror, a good rule of thumb is to make it centered at the height of your face. The height of a picture can vary according to style. Look on the back of your picture. Is there a wire or simply a notch to hang it from? Make a mark with a pencil at the desired height, keeping in mind that the play of the wire may change where your nail needs to go.

4. Put the picture down, and position the nail over the marking. Hammer it in, leaving about ¼ inch of the nail exposed to hold the picture.

5. Hang your picture.

6. Although I always tend to eyeball it, I would recommend putting a small level at the top of your picture to make sure that it's straight.

- There is no need to drill a pilot hole for nails.
- Purchase a picture-hanging kit. This will come with various nails and hooks to attach most pictures to walls. It also contains wire to put on the back of pictures that are not already equipped.

Hanging a Heavy Picture or Mirror

A typical "heavy" picture or mirror will range in weight from about forty to a hundred pounds. The way to hang one is very similar to the project described above, except that your hardware will change. Instead of a small picture-hanging nails, you will need heavy-duty nails, wire, and hooks that will support the weight of the picture.

If the picture or mirror weighs more than one hundred pounds, you will need to buy extremely heavy-duty hardware. It's best to check with someone at the hardware store for the manufacturer's recommendations.

TUFF METER: 7

TIMER: 1 hour

TUFF TOOLS: Bathroom scale, pencil, hammer, level, tape measure, wire cutters, screwdriver, drill with ⅛-inch drill bit and screwdriver attachment

SHOPPING LIST: Heavy-duty picture wire ($3.89), picture-hanging nails ($1.99–$3.99), heavy-duty D-rings ($1.89/package of 2)

TOTAL PRICE: $7.77

$25/hour, plus materials

How to hang a heavy picture or mirror on drywall:

1. How much does your picture weigh? You must find out before you proceed. All wire, hardware, and picture-hanging kits will come with a rating based on weight. The best way to determine the weight is with your very own bathroom scale. Sure, you may be staying away from it for different reasons, but you will want to come back to it today. Stand on the scale with the picture in your hands. How much do you weigh? Now set the picture down and get back on the scale. How much do you weigh now? The difference is the weight of the picture.

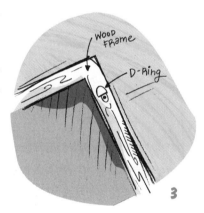

2. If the picture already has wire and rings on the back for hanging, skip to step 12. If it doesn't, follow the next steps.

3. Take heavy-duty D-rings, which look like little Ds, and attach them to the back of the picture frame. Make sure you are attaching them to wood. Put them on either side of the picture. You will want them to be two-thirds of the way up, and about an inch from the edge.

4. Mark one side where you will attach the D-ring.

5. Take your tape measure and measure the length from the top of the painting to the mark. Measure down on the other side and make another mark for the D-ring on the other side.

6. Drill pilot holes for your D-ring installation. Be careful not to go entirely through the wood.

7. Attach the D-rings with the screws provided. You will want to tilt the rings at almost a 45-degree angle, since this is what the nails will rest on.

8. Cut the heavy-duty wire with a wire cutter. You will want to make it about double the length of the picture.

9. Put one end through one D-ring and bring it back, wrapping it around itself.

10. Pull it fairly tight to the other D-ring, and do the same. You can leave a little slack.

11. Cut off any excess wire with the wire cutters.

12. Now decide where you would like your picture to go on the wall. Mark it lightly with a pencil.

13. Find the nearest stud to your designated area.

14. On that stud, hold the picture up again to get the desired height. With a mirror, a good rule of thumb is to center it at the height of your face. The height of a picture can vary according to style. Make a mark with your pencil at your desired height, keeping in mind that the wire you just installed will change the positioning of your nail slightly.

15. For a small heavy picture, all you need is one nail. For a larger (and heavier) picture, you will need to add more. Find the two studs on either side of your center mark. They should be 16 inches to either side. You can

choose one or both to put a nail into. Use your level to make sure you are marking the area at the same height.

16. Put the picture down and position the nail over the marking. Make sure you are using a large, heavy-duty nail. Hammer it in, leaving about ¼ inch of the nail exposed to hold the picture. If your heavy-duty picture-hanging kit came with hangers, attach them to your nail before you hammer it in.

17. Hang your picture. You may need to enlist a helper for this one. If it's too heavy, don't overdo it.

18. Although you can adjust a smaller picture (eyeball or level it), the two or more nails you put in the wall will level this larger picture (providing you made them level).

REFERENCE

Maintenance Schedule

There are many disasters that occur in the home that can be quite easily avoided if you know what to do and what to look for. Use this as your yearlong guide to keeping your house in tip-top shape. Although this chart is geared for home owners, many of the same issues apply to apartments, so don't overlook things you could do to have a happy residence anywhere!

I've divided the maintenance schedule into the four seasons, plus an additional section of things to check at the beginning of *every* season. Use this as your guide and road map. Photocopy these pages and use them every year, filling in the notes section. This will not only allow you to stay on top of your home, it will provide a great record for the future (even when you sell your home).

Perform these checks at the *beginning* of every season. It will help you enjoy your home through every season of the year.

Things to check at the beginning of EVERY season:

At the beginning of each season, you should inspect the following items. Checking these simple things every few months will help prevent serious damage to your house, or even worse, your loved ones.

WHAT TO CHECK	WHAT TO DO	NOTES
Fire extinguishers	Make sure they are fully charged and have been properly stored in accessible locations.	
Smoke detectors/carbon monoxide detectors	Push the button on each of these, and hold it down until the alarm sounds. This will also set off others in the home. Make sure batteries are in good working order. Change the batteries every time you change your clocks.	
Clothes dryer	Check (and clean) the exit vents to make sure they are free of lint and debris. Check behind the dryer for any clothes that may have fallen back there.	
Washing machine	Check the washing machine hoses to make sure they are tight. Make sure they don't have any cracks or bubbles in the line that could break.	
Bathroom	Check the caulking and grout for any possible cracks, discoloration, or mold. Check for leaks under or around the sink and around the toilet.	
Kitchen	Check the grout and the caulking for cracks, discoloration, and mold. Check around and under the sink for leaks.	
All visible pipes, supply lines, and shutoff valves.	Check all of these that you can see— this means in your attic, basement, under sinks, outside, behind toilets, etc. Make sure there are no leaks, that supply lines are in good order, and that the shutoff valves can turn on and off.	

WHAT TO CHECK	WHAT TO DO	NOTES
GFCI receptacles	Push the "test" and "reset" buttons on each of these around your home. This will test the mechanism.	
Air-conditioning filters	Check the a/c filter. Replace if needed.	
Electrical cords	Check all electrical cords to make sure there is no damage. If there is, replace or fix immediately.	
Molding/baseboards	Inspect all molding found near the floor and around window- and doorjambs. Make sure they are in good shape (not rotting and not loose).	
Flooring	Check all the flooring in the home and see if it needs replacing or repairs.	

The Seasons:

Winter: Winter is a *very* important checklist to complete. So much can go wrong in your home during this time, due to Mother Nature, and you want to make sure that you are prepared *before* disaster strikes. Also, the fall months bring just what it sounds like it would—falling leaves and debris. When the winter weather kicks up and brings rain and snow, it will be hard for you to keep things in good working order if you neglect this winter checklist.

WHAT TO CHECK	WHAT TO DO	NOTES
Gutters	This is a big one. Gutters can get filled with leaves and debris and clog up when the rain or snow comes. Get out there, inspect them all, and clean them out.	
Weather stripping	Check around all the doors and windows to make sure the seal is in good condition and that no draft or water is present. Through the heat of summer and the wind of fall, weather stripping can take a beating.	

WHAT TO CHECK	WHAT TO DO	NOTES
Doors/windows	In addition to the weather stripping, check the condition of each door and window. Check to make sure they close properly and have no damage or cracks.	
Roof	Clear all debris off the roof and check for any missing shingles. You will want to make sure the roof is in good order before the weather turns bad.	

Spring: Spring is another time for *very* important inspections. The destruction that winter brought for the past few months needs your attention so that the damage doesn't become a hazard or danger.

WHAT TO CHECK	WHAT TO DO	NOTES
Attic	Check the attic for leaks and moisture.	
Basement	Check the basement for leaks and moisture.	
Roof	Check the roof for leaks, missing shingles, and any damage winter might have brought.	
Chimney	Your fireplace was probably used a little more last season than all the other seasons combined. Check to make sure there is no debris in the chimney and it is free of buildup. Have it cleaned by a professional.	
Gutters	Make sure they are free of debris and have not been damaged by the winter months. Make sure they drain correctly.	
Fans (bathrooms, attic, etc.)	Check these fans to make sure they are running properly. Take off vents to assure they are free of debris.	

Summer: It's hot, it's fun, it's vacation time, but don't go on vacation without giving your home a little love.

WHAT TO CHECK	WHAT TO DO	NOTES
Windows/doors	Check for any possible dampness or dry rot. They probably received a lot of wet weather over the past few months and could have sustained damage.	
Exterior walls	Check your siding, stucco, or any outside surface of the home. Check for cracking or crumbling. Check for peeling paint or areas in need of touch-up.	
All concrete surfaces (driveways, walkways, etc.)	Check for cracks, uneven surfaces, or areas that are starting to crumble. Repair as soon as possible so the problem doesn't get bigger.	
Foundation	Look all around your home's foundation. Look for cracks and repair them immediately. If the soil of your landscape has been washed away (therefore causing water to puddle at your foundation) add soil to slope it away from the house.	
Air-conditioning unit	Make sure it is in good condition and working properly. Make sure air is blowing from all vents (and therefore ducts have not been pulled away in the attic). Check and replace filter if needed. It will be working harder than any time of the year, so this may be a good time to replace it.	
A/C vent covers	Make sure they are all clean. It's a good idea to take them all off and clean them with soap and water. Since they will have a lot of air blowing through them soon, you don't want dust blowing everywhere, too. This also allows for full, uncompromised airflow.	

Fall: Back to school, back from vacation, back to business. Fall is a great time to make sure that your house is ready for the big winter ahead.

WHAT TO CHECK	WHAT TO DO	NOTES
Water heater	Completely drain the tank to start over. This rids it of sediment and possible residual bacteria that could get into your water.	
Gutters	Make sure they are clean of debris and are not damaged, including in any joints.	
Heat vent covers	See *A/C vent covers*.	
Fireplace/chimney	You are getting ready to use this a lot, so make sure it is clear of debris.	

Dictionary

Girls, these terms will help you become a true Tuff Chick. Consider this your own "homegirl" dictionary.

Blue painter's tape: A type of masking tape that you will find in the painting section of the hardware store. It comes in a variety of widths and allows you to tape off sections that you do not wish to paint (such as baseboards, moldings, windowsills, etc.).

Boyfriend: Can be trained to carry out instructions or to help when you just need that extra little bit of muscle; recommended for paint and/or plumbing jobs, and when a door has to be taken off its hinges.

Brackets: Metal or wood angled strips with slots that anchor the shelves.

Caulk/Caulking: "Caulk" is one of those words that can be both noun and verb. As the verb, "to caulk" means to make watertight or airtight by filling or sealing; you can caulk a pipe joint, for example, or the cracks between tiles and around faucets. "Caulk" (also "caulking") as the noun is the (mostly white or clear) goop that is used as the filler or sealant.

Cement: The component that hardens masonry mixtures when water is added. It is a combination of lime, silica, alumina, iron, and gypsum.

Ceramic tile: Usually made from clay, ceramic tile is finished by kiln firing. Made in many shapes and sizes, it can be glazed or unglazed. Tiles are usually set in a cement or a mortar-type mixture. Generally used in bathtub and shower enclosures and on countertops.

Circuit breaker: Automatic switch that shuts off the flow of electricity if stressed or overloaded. Literally creates a "break" in the circuit.

Concrete: A mixture of cement, gravel, and sand.

Cornice: A decorative framework (molding) to conceal curtain fixtures at the top of a window casing. Also, a molding at the corner between the ceiling and the top of a wall.

Cutting: When used in reference to painting, this means "edging" paint, or starting in the corners and the outer edges of a wall with a paintbrush, bringing in the paint a few inches so that it is easy to roll.

Door sweep: The weather stripping that lies at the bottom of your exterior door and keeps out creepy crawlies.

Dowel: A piece of wood driven into a wall, door, or cabinet to act as an anchor for nails or screws. Can be any size round piece of wood (e.g., closet dowel).

Drywall: A wall or ceiling constructed of a prefabricated material, such as plasterboard. The term can also simply refer to plasterboard, wallboard, Sheetrock, and gypsum.

Ex-boyfriend: Only to be used in an emergency, and not without known risks, exes are nevertheless excellent tools for those tougher jobs when friend, boyfriend, or checkbooks are not an option.

Faceplate covers: The covers on an electrical wall switch.

Fiberglass tape: Woven fiberglass fabric with a pressure-sensitive adhesive system on one or both sides.

Fuse box: A metal box that is usually 12×18 inches in size, however they range from as small as 5×7 inches to as large as 20 by 40 inches. Holds all the fuses for your house/apartment.

GFCI (ground fault circuit interrupter): An inexpensive electrical device that detects even small faults in electrical current movement and cuts power to prevent electrical shocks and/or fires. Found around sinks or water sources.

Grout: A cement-based powder that is mixed with water. Grout fills the area between tiles to not only give a nice, finished look, but to also create a watertight seal.

Husband: Excellent for holding a ladder or supporting you in your time of need.

Induction lamp: More expensive than other light sources, this newer technology has no filament or electrodes and therefore a much longer life and minimal maintenance costs.

Jamb: A pair of vertical posts or pieces that together form the sides of a door, window frame, or fireplace.

Joint compound: Another goopy substance that fills joints between drywall.

Joist: Any of the wood, steel, or concrete beams supporting a floor or ceiling.

Lath: A thin strip of wood or metal, usually nailed in rows and used as backing for plaster, shingles, slates, or tiles.

Masonry: Any building of structures from individual units laid in and bound together by mortar. The materials most commonly used are brick, stone, concrete block, glass block, and tile.

Mold: Growth of fungus, usually in a damp, dark area.

Molding: An embellishment used to decorate or finish a surface, such as the wall or ceiling of a room.

Muriatic acid: Also, hydrochloric acid. A strongly corrosive liquid solution of hydrogen chloride.

Peephole: The little looking glass located in the center of an exterior door that allows you to see who's at your doorstep without you having to open the door.

Pilot hole: A small-diameter, predrilled hole that guides a nail or screw. Also used to guide a drill or other cutting tool for making a larger hole.

Plumb: Vertically straight.

Power strip: A row of outlets that allows you to plug in more appliances from one wall outlet. Not to be confused with a surge protector, which can look almost identical. See *surge protector*.

Primer: An undercoat of sealant used to prepare a surface for painting or a similar process.

Soffit: The underside of a part of a building (such as of an arch, overhang, beam, etc.).

Strike plate: The flat metal plate attached to the doorjamb; a lock set's latch or bolt strikes this plate to keep a door closed.

Stucco: A durable finish for exterior walls, usually composed of cement, sand, and lime, and applied while wet.

Stud (Wall stud): Not to be confused with a cute cowboy, a stud (or wall stud) is a wooden 2 × 4- or 2 × 6-inch plank of wood. Studs make up the inside frame of a wall. Heavy shelves or pictures are most secure when mounted to wall studs.

Surge protector: A strip of power outlets with built-in protection against power surges (not to be confused with a simple power strip; see *power strip*).

Three-way switch: Single light controlled from two locations.

Trim: All sections that add detail to your home; found around windows, doors, soffits, fasciae, corner boards, etc.

Wall anchors: These come in plastic and metal and are designed to screw into a wall, particularly where no walls studs can be used. These allow you to hang heavier items that would normal pull through drywall.

Weather stripping: The small lining around your doors that prevents drafts and leaks from entering your home. See illustration, page 112.

Wood filler: A substance that can be used to fill knotholes and deep dents in wood that will be painted.

Glossary

Girls, look below. I not only give you a picture of the tool, but also the common terms that these tools are referred to as. Between the job site, the hardware store, and your friends, you will hear a variety of terms for the same tool. I tried to list all the terms I've ever heard of for each tool.

Backsaw: Saw that is reinforced by a metal band along its back edge. An old-fashioned hand saw.

Belt sander: A power sander that works with the sandpaper on a "belt" that goes around continuously. It's a loop of sandpaper moved at a high speed by an electric motor. It can be handheld or upright for larger, floor jobs.

Carpenter's square: A trick for new players, this is actually a triangle. In carpentry, a square or set square is a guide for establishing right angles (ninety-degree angles), usually made of metal and in the shape of a right triangle.

Caulking gun: Yep, it shoots caulk from the tube. Good for larger jobs, it helps you have better control of the goop, allowing a "bead" of material to be applied to cracks and seams.

Chisel: A tool with a flat steel blade with a cutting edge. Chisels can be used by tapping lightly with a mallet, or they can be worked by hand.

Circular saw: A metal disc or blade with saw teeth on the edge as well as on the machine that causes the disc to spin. It is a tool for cutting wood or other materials and may be hand-held or table-mounted.

Crowbar, prybar, flat bar: A heavy iron lever with one end shaped as a wedge. Used to pry.

Drill bit: The cutting or boring pieces that fit inside the drill's tip. They are interchangable and come in a variety of sizes.

Drywall saw: A short, stout handsaw used to make long, straight cuts in drywall panels.

Electric drill, cordless drill, power drill, screw gun, battery drill, power drill: A power tool that works as a screw gun, or is used for making holes in hard materials. Comes with interchangeable heads for a variety of applications. The head section works in an orbital method, going round and round at a very rapid pace, controlled by your finger on the trigger.

Flat-head screwdriver: Just like it sounds—a screwdriver with a flat head, used for screws with a single slit across the top.

Float: A handheld tool used to finish a concrete or masonry surface.

Hammer: If you don't know what this is by now, there's probably no hope for you. Good for hitting things such as nails.

Hand plane: Wood surfacing tool with sharp blades on the bottom. Used to shave off the outer sides of wood to create a smooth or square finish.

Hand sander, power sander, electric sander, orbital sander, finishing sander, smoother: A small, handheld power tool used for sanding wood. Can vibrate side to side or in an orbital fashion to rough up and smooth the surface of wood.

Heat gun: Kind of like a blow-dryer, this electrical appliance features a tapered nozzle for directing hot air onto objects, and is used to soften materials when cutting, shaping, or for force-drying adhesives.

Hole saw: A small cylindrical attachment for a power drill that consists of a circular saw blade, used to cut holes.

Hot glue gun: Like the other goop (aka, caulking) gun, this does exactly what it suggests—heats up glue and pushes it out the nozzle of the gun. It goes on hot and liquidlike and hardens as it cools. Hurts *a lot* when you get it on your hand because it sticks and burns. Ouch!

Knee kicker: A carpet installation tool used to push carpet into corners or against walls. You literally kick it with your knee, as the tool name might suggest, so that you get a little more stretch out of carpet.

Level: A hand tool for checking that any piece is perfectly horizontal or vertical.

Nail sinker, nail set: A small shaft of metal with a blunt point used to set a nail below the surface of wood. Put it over a small nail and tap it in with a hammer.

Paintbrush: A brush for applying paint. Comes in a variety of shapes and sizes. How to choose a good one?

Paint roller: A cylinder that has an absorbent surface used to apply paint.

Paint scraper: Like a bigger, often triangular, version of a putty knife, this flat-bladed tool is a must-have for painting jobs if you're taking back old paint. Can also be used as a trowel for small jobs.

Phillips screwdriver: Just like it sounds—a screwdriver with a Phillips head, used for screws with crosshead slits across the top. Actually developed by a guy named Henry F. Phillips back in the 1930s to help aid the use of power screwdrivers. It gives the screwdriver more stability by keeping it on track.

Pipe cutter: A hand tool for cutting pipes.

Pliers: A gripping hand tool with two hinged arms and (usually) serrated jaws. Needle-nose pliers have long, narrow jaws used to get into small places (kind of like large tweezers).

Putty knife: A flat-bladed tool used to mix and apply putty, and to fill cracks and holes with spackling compound.

Reciprocating saw: A power saw that looks like a shark where the blades move back and forth (a reciprocating blade) to provide cutting. Resembles an electric knife for cutting turkey at Thanksgiving.

Rubber mallet: Looks like a cross between a hammer and a sledgehammer, only with a rubber head. It's used to apply the force of a blow without applying damage to the surface.

Sanding blocks: A block of wood covered in sandpaper, used to sand down a wood surface. These are easy to make (or buy).

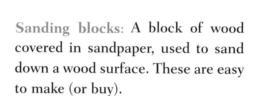

Screwdriver: A hand tool used for turning screws. Two main types: Phillips and flat-head.

Sewer snake, snaker, auger: A flexible metal rod with a spiral hook or ball at the end, long enough to reach deep into a drain-pipe. Used to break up a clog in a pipe, it is a boring tool. It winds and unwinds to desired length.

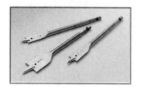

Spade bit, paddle bit: Like it suggests, an attachment for your power drill that looks like a miniature spade or paddle; used for quickly drilling holes in wood.

Stud finder: Us girls? Actually, a stud finder is a small tool used to locate the position of the stud behind a wallboard. This allows you to know where you can safetly hang a picture or heavy object on the wall.

Tape measure, pocket tape: A tape of steel, cloth, paper, etc., marked off with inches, feet, centimeter, etc., for taking measurements.

Tin snips, aviation snips, metal shears: A hand shear–like tool for cutting aluminum and sheet metal.

Trowel: A steel or plastic tool with a flat, triangular-shaped blade or surface that makes smoothing concrete, drywall, and other surfaces easy.

Utility knife, box cutter, retractable knife: A tool containing a blade usually between 5 and 7 inches long, and used to cut a variety of materials, including vinyl sheet and vinyl tile during installation.

Whisk broom: A bundle of straws attached to a long handle, used to sweep.

Wire brush: Like it sounds, it is a small brush made with hard-bristled wires. Good for all sorts of cleaning and unclogging.

Wire cutter: An edge tool used by electricians to cut wire.

Wire stripper: Tool designed to remove the insulation from a wire without damaging the wire itself.

Wrench, spanner: A hand tool used to turn nuts, bolts, or any other hard-to-turn items.

Index

Garbage disposals, 172–173,
191
Gas main, 18
Gate valves, 172
GFCI (ground-fault circuit
interrupter), 16, 18, 19
defined, 287
inspection of, 281
Globe valves, 172
Gloss/high-gloss finish, 63
Grout
defined, 46, 287
discolored, 46–47
replacing, 48–49
types of, 46
Gutters, 248
cleaning, 147–148
inspection of, 281, 282,
284
patching leaks, 148–149
Gypsum (*see* Drywall)

H

Halls, 23
Hammers, 292
Handles, cabinet, 135–136
Hand planes, 292
Hand sanders, 292
HAP (hire a professional), 3
cost estimate, 4, 27
questions to ask, 326–28
Hardwood floors
eliminating squeaks,
93–94
removing stains, 92–93
repairing holes, 88–89
sanding, 89–92
stains and finishes, 86–88
Heat guns, 292
Heat stripping, 76–77
Hinges, loose, 107–109,
137–138
Hole saws, 292
Hose bib valves, 172
Hot glue guns, 292

I

Induction lamps, defined,
287
Instructions, following, 14

J

Jamb, defined, 287
Joint compound, defined, 287
Joist, defined, 288

K

Kitchens
fire prevention, 226–227
inspection of, 18, 280
Kiyosaki, Robert, 9
Knee kickers, 293
Knobs, cabinet, 135–136

L

Lacquer, 62, 86
Latches, sticky, 119–120
Lath, defined, 288
Laundry rooms, 20–21
Laws, 24–26
Leaks
gutter, 148–149
laundry room, 20–21
sink, 17
toilet, 188–191
Levels, 293
Licenses, 27
Light fixture problems and
solutions, 205–206
Lighting, 199–200, 236–239
(*see also* Electrical
repairs)
Light switches, changing,
202–204
Locks (*see* Bolts and locks)

M

Maintenance schedule, 23,
279–284
Masonry, defined, 288

Spanners, 295
Spontaneous combustion, 229
Spot damage, in carpet, 95
Square sanders, 91, 92
Squeaks, eliminating, 93–94
Stain removal
    carpet, 95
    hardwood floors, 92–93
Stem faucets, 177
Stop orders, 25
Strike plates, 234
    adjusting, 120, 123
    defined, 289
Stucco
    defined, 149, 289
    repairing, 149–152
Stud finders, 265, 268, 294
Studs, 265, 267, 268, 270
    defined, 289
Success, tips for, 12–15
Supply lines, 20–21, 280
Surge protectors
    defined, 289
    installing, 216–217

T

Tape measures, 294
Tap repair, 177–181
Tears, in vinyl flooring, 100–102
Termites, 158, 160, 161
Three-way switch, defined, 289
Tile flooring, 102–103
Timer switches, 215
Tin snips, 295
Toilets
    childproofing, 244
    clogged, 185–186
    leaky, 188–191
    problems and solutions, 190
    running, 186–187
    seat replacement, 182–184

Tools, 4, 8
    photographs and descriptions of, 290–295
    quality of, 14
Trim, defined, 289
Trim paint, 65
Trim surfaces, preparing exterior, 157–158
Trowels, 295
Tub drains, 175–177
Tuff Chix, Inc., 11

U

Utility knives, 295

V

Valves, 171–172
Varnishes, 62
    choice of, 86–88
Veneer, 85
Vinyl flooring, 18, 98–101
Vinyl siding, 165–166

W

Walkways, 283
Wall anchors, defined, 254, 289
Wallboard (*see* Drywall)
Wall-mounted doorstops, 129, 131
Wallpaper
    bubbles in, 53
    patching, 54–55
    removing, 55–57
Walls (*see* Drywall; Exterior walls; Wallpaper)
Washers, 177–179
Washing machines, 280
    hoses, 191–193
Water-based latex paint, 61, 62
Water heaters, 284
Water main, 18
Water pressure, 17, 181
Wattage ratings, 217–221
Wax ring, replacing, 188–189, 191